Life is a Road, the Soul is a Motorcycle

Life is a Road, the Soul is a Motorcycle

Daniel Brian Meyer

iUniverse, Inc.
New York Lincoln Shanghai

Life is a Road, the Soul is a Motorcycle

iUniverse, Inc.

For information address:
iUniverse, Inc.
2021 Pine Lake Road, Suite 100
Lincoln, NE 68512
www.iuniverse.com

ISBN: 0-595-26990-7 (pbk)
ISBN: 0-595-65642-0 (cloth)

Printed in the United States of America

For Mom, who taught me to write.
For Dad, who taught me to ride.
And for my Wife, who inspires me to do both.

The purpose of man is to live, not to exist.

—Jack London

Contents

Acknowledgements

Cover Design by Dan Peters.
Interior Illustrations by Ron Lee.

I wish to thank Ron Lee for his excellent illustrations and patient tolerance of such phrases as, "Draw, damn you!"; Dan Peters for truly capturing the spirit of the book with his cover design; My friends at the VRCC (f6rider.com), BBR (bigbikeriders.com), the XS forums (xs11.com and the Yahoo group allxs11), and at the Yahoo group BikerSouls for all the critique, suggestions, encouragement, assistance, and many hours of fine riding and companionship.

To my life-long friend James Randles, who has accompanied me on more miles than I can recall—words fail me, so I'll simply say thanks for being there. Here's to many more miles yet to travel.

Finally, to all the people I have met and have yet to meet on my various travels; keep it safe and keep it positive.

I'll see you on the road.

Introduction

Sitting astride "The Dragon," my massive F6 Valkyrie cruiser, something caught my eye and I paused before starting the bike and leaving the gas station. Memories stirred as I watched a father and his young son dismounting their motorcycle in the parking lot of the nearby restaurant. As the boy removed his helmet, the grin I knew would surely be there shone brightly for the entire world to see.

As the father removed his own helmet, I could see what I expected there too. We traded nods as he listened to his son excitedly explain some aspect of their ride. His face was an interesting combination of emotions. Satisfaction for a well executed ride, pleasure at his son's obvious enjoyment, and a little anxiety that he was so responsible for something so precious to himself. Wanting to protect his son, but knowing he must expose the boy to the world in order for him to someday become a man. This is a look I know well from my childhood. I saw it many times on my Dad, but never really understood completely until long after I had become an adult.

My earliest coherent memories are of motorcycling as a 10-year-old riding behind my Dad on his 1970's era Honda 350. Just the two of us, rumbling, curving, and swooping down the road. Flying really. The wind and motion, sights and smells, all vividly experienced and permanently etched into my being. I was at that fortunate age before I became too "cool" to hang around with him, and we commuted to all the events that a dad is required to take his sons to. Boy Scouts and baseball, camping trips and family visits. Hot, cold, rain, and dust. If we could, we rode. We traveled the highways and explored the back roads. We went places just to go places. I can remember several times when we stopped and helped stranded motorists. Life was good when I was on a bike with my Dad.

Even at that age I was disappointed when we had to take the "cage", the motorcyclist's slang for a car or truck. Even then I knew there was something special about motorcycles. I already realized that there was some connection between the man and his machine. And I knew that motorcycles are far more than just transportation. As a passenger I could feel it a little bit and as a son I could see it strongly in my Dad. It was obvious that together, the man and the machine were far more then the sum of their parts. And it was obvious that apart they were somehow, just a little bit, *incomplete*.

As the time and the miles have flown by, I have found the world to be an interesting and magical place. Journeying near and far on the various bikes I have had over the years, I have reaffirmed this again and again. There is plenty of the mundane aspect of the world too; I feel it is unfortunate that most people spend all their time there. But the magic exists if they know how to see it. There is plenty for all, and they will find it if they look for it.

I stood there for a moment recalling my many travels over the years. The sights I have seen, the people I have met, and the magic I have experienced. All were palely reflected in the eyes of the boy in the parking lot. All had been reflected in the eyes of the 10-year-old I had been, and all helped foresee the man I would become. Sitting there on "The Dragon" I realized how important to my *self* those experiences were. How much I would have missed without them. I resolved then to write them down, to try to chronicle the journeys, and to try to show this wonderful world to those that were ready to see it.

This book is the result. What follows is a series of short stories chronicling some of my journeys. They are best read in the order presented. Some explore the "where", some explore the "who", and some the "why." All lead me to where I finally realized what I had truly known all along. What the young boy standing there with his father also knew. What all of us really know somewhere deep inside, even though as adults we have somehow mostly forgotten.

What we have forgotten is that it doesn't matter where we are going in this world or in our lives. The destination is not what's significant.

It is the journey that matters.

The journey *is* the destination.

I took one last, lingering look, aching a bit as I watched the son hug his father before they headed into the restaurant. I took a deep breath and let it out slowly. I pushed the start button on "The Dragon" and the superb machine rumbled smoothly to life.

As I waited for a break in traffic I mumbled to myself, "Yes," while reaching deep into my soul to see if I still *knew.*

I did. I was certain. "Yes, I *do* remember."

The traffic broke for a moment. I grinned, "The Dragon" roared, and we were gone.

The Bet

Ah, the essence of youth. The time when we do not require a reason, or a justification for every significant action or challenge we tackle. We would do well to remember some of that in our adult lives. When is the last time you went on a journey, just to go on the journey?

Ride Report: "I Get a New Traveling Companion"
Alternate Title: "Who Let the Cat Out of the Bag?"
Title if the wife (acquired later) named it: "Honey...You're an Idiot"
Title if best friend named it: "Well, OK. Two Cokes."

My first coherent thought of the day was, *"This is a desolate place."* The second thought was along the lines of, *"What the HELL am I doing out here?"* The third...I think...was something about trading my soul for a breakfast. Probably not good.

I was rocketing through the New Mexico desert's predawn light. My only source of company and comfort in this dark and desolate landscape was the machine I was astride. The big Suzuki was howling at wide-open throttle, singing in ecstasy at doing what it was created for. I was cold, exhausted, hungry, and lonely. I also had a deadline. I had to get back to Dallas...and soon, although I really wasn't sure exactly why.

Suzuki made two models of the 750 in 1981. The "E" model, which had a more squared off, more modern look and a larger gas tank, and the "GL" which had the "cruiser" look. Due to a moment of weakness, and a really good deal, I had one of each. The problem with these bikes was that although they were absolutely beautiful machines, mechanically they had a very limited lifespan. They would run, and run well…right up to a certain point, then you pushed them over and left them beside the highway where they had left you. I had selected the 750E model for this mission, mainly due to its larger capacity gas tank. Extra stops were a luxury I could not afford on this trip. It also had hard saddlebags that I had gotten from a bone yard and made to fit. The slightly wider seat was an added and fortunate benefit.

Several relevant facts should be revealed so folks do not misunderstand (or do misunderstand…whatever their pleasure). First, I was a *lot* younger than I am now, thus the apparently foolish nature of the errand. And second, any perceived "slowness" or inexperience on my part is probably due to the fact that…well…I was inexperienced…but mainly that I had left Dallas less than 24 hours ago. Yep, Dallas to Pikes Peak and back into the New Mexico Desert in about 18 hours. On a 750. 18 hours of high speed travel on any motorcycle will dull anyone's brain. Most probably wonder why at this point—let's just say it was on a bet, and the only cargo I was carrying back with me was a set of official Pike's Peak salt and pepper shakers, and a Park Service receipt saying I had driven to the top. And I was cursing the day *Smokey and the Bandit* came out.

Riding is the point, yes?

Anyway, headed back I was hauling down Interstate 25. I was supposed to catch US 64/87 in Raton, New Mexico and cut across to Dalhart, Texas. I had apparently gotten into "cruise" mode and it finally dawned on me that even though the last town I gassed up in was Raton, I was still hauling south on Interstate 25 at a very high rate of speed. Kept driving for another 10 minutes or so while my brain laboriously ground out possible actions to take. *Hmmmm.* Whipped out the map and found some back roads and zipped out into the flat desert plains.

Watch out for the sand traps if you ever do this. Apparently this area flash floods during heavy but infrequent rains, and the places where these torrents cross the roads are not bridged—they are just a concrete road about 400 feet long that is lower and narrower than the regular blacktop road. It is what we would call a "wash" here in Texas. Would not be a problem to drive through, except for the 6–12 inches of sand accumulated there from the last deluge. Real bitch to drive a 750 street bike through, especially if it looks like regular road in your headlight and you enter it at over 70 mph. Lots of mule deer out here too, especially when you hit a sand trap at 70 mph and suddenly end up "off-road". The deer are easy to spot though, because there is absolutely nothing else out here.

The sun finally came up so life got a little better—it gets *cold* out here at night, even in August. Finally I came to the rather fundamental and somehow surprising conclusion that there is only so long a man can go without taking a piss. I had to find a place to stop, the leathers suddenly had to come off anyway—it gets *hot* out here in August, even if it is just after sun-up. I belatedly realize that all I have had to eat in about the last 20 hours is some undetermined number of Twinkies and probably an equal number of Ding-dongs, all washed down by massive quantities of Coca-Cola. I got pretty good at doing this while I was pumping the gas, like I said—stops were a luxury I could not afford. Ever eat a Twinkie in a full-face helmet?

Looked closely at my map…and again at my watch…and incredulously back at the map. My fuzzy brain eventually ground to the conclusion that I had gained some time. Apparently the lack of observed speed limits on the back-roads had enabled me to bring Einstein's relativity equations into play despite the sand traps. Had to be, because I know the 750 can't really go that fast…um…well…maybe. Always seemed to me as if it needed another gear. Anyway, I was ready to kill for breakfast, and some of the many mule deer I was dodging were starting to look pretty tasty. I decided I could afford a stop for a real, sit-down meal.

By this time I had reached some roads I recognized, namely US 87, so I stopped at the first town and gassed up. Here is a little uncertainty…I am pretty sure I was still in New Mexico…but honestly, sometime in the night I had entered a time-warp and really had not a lot of clues as to what I was doing or where I really was. I just knew I had to get back to Dallas. Anyway, I can state with reasonable certainty that I was either in Clayton, New Mexico or Texline, Texas—I hope. After fueling and resisting the somehow very strong urge to violently destroy the Hostess display in the store, I moved the bike across the street to "Debbie's", which was advertising "Foo" on her sign...the "d" long having vanished. I figured I could use some "Foo". The place looked pretty good. Several truckers were parked there and they don't eat at crappy places. There were enough other miscellaneous type of vehicles scattered about that I was reasonably sure I would be given a table. Also, and maybe this was the deciding factor, it had a tree to park the bike under. Shade is a scarce commodity out here and the Suzuki "E" tended to shoot gas into your crotch if you left it in the sun for very long with a full tank. Suzukis can be testy at times. Works pretty good for getting rid of jock itch, but not really highly recommended, particularly if you are four or five hundred miles from the nearest accessible shower.

I stumbled in and sat myself. Without a word "Debbie" or her substitute handed me a menu and a cup of coffee. Normally I don't drink coffee, but this I needed. Good place. Good coffee.

She finally asked, "What'll you have Hon?"

I was somewhat surprised to find that I could not read the menu. Seems it just would not stop vibrating. I even tried laying it flat on the table and holding it down with both hands. Nothing seemed to work. When I started to weight the corners of the menu down with my coffee cup and the sugar dispenser, all the while staring intently at the table she asked, "You all right?" ("You all" was said as one word...but was somehow different from the Texas "Y'all" that means...well...*y'all*).

Debbie was definitely *not* vibrating (I don't think I could take it) so finally I gave up and ordered what I was hungry for, "A dozen scrambled eggs, a half-pound of bacon, toast, jam, and iced tea."

To Debbie's credit she did not comment. She did not even blink. "Sure thing Hon."

Exactly six minutes later I had the biggest and best breakfast I had ever had in my life. Like I said...good place. I polished it off in record time. The bill was just over six bucks. Guess I can hang onto my soul.

For future reference, this was the only place or time in the entire journey that the bike was out of my site for more than a few seconds. That is important later.

Back on the road again. Alive again. Wow. What a difference a good breakfast can make. Jamming down the road. The tape player was dying again. This was the last of the batteries too. Did not really matter, I had listened to the same auto-reversed tape for about 15 hours now. Was beginning to hate REO Speedwagon, and that for me is a really bad sign. Interesting phenomenon observed here...when the batteries start to go dead the tape, and thus the music, slows down. I did not notice. Magically, the motorcycle speeds up. The way I could tell the batteries were dying was that my hand began aching from trying to twist the throttle past its stop.

Somewhere north of Amarillo I threw the completely dead tape player at a pick-up full of teenagers that tried to run me off the road...twice. No big loss, and all in a good cause. One tape player for one windshield. Seemed fair to me. Really cooking now...and not just speed. It is hot out here. Somewhat south of Amarillo and a gas stop later my bike let out the most ungodly howl that I have ever heard from a machine. Something in the rear was going to let go. Pulled over and checked around. No unusual heat, nothing seemed loose. *Hmmmm.* Put it up on the work stand and exercised the drive line. Nothing unusual, chain tension ok. I stand up and turn 360 degrees looking at the horizon. There is nothing out here, and no cars have passed since I stopped. No real choice. Time to go on.

I get another 10 or 15 minutes before the noise starts again. I play with the bike a little this time. The sound varies in pitch and volume, but does not seem to be related to speed or throttle position. Definitely coming from the rear. This is really weird. I have always done all my own wrenching, and I have never heard anything like this.

About this time a "Picnic Area" shows up beside the road. In Texas a "Rest Area" has a rest-room, a "Picnic Area" can mean anything from tables and benches to a gravel parking lot. This one had a single table and a bench. There were several other covers where there were supposed to be tables, but there was just an empty concrete pad under each. There were several army trucks and an RV parked in the lot. With a sigh of relief I pulled into the shade under one of the covers and stopped. I was astounded when I turned off the engine and the noise continued.

Quick diagnoses revealed that the noise was decidedly animal in nature, and was coming from my left hard bag. I tried to open it but what looked like a stick had been shoved in the lock and broken off. The bag had not been locked, but this was the type of latch that had the keyhole in the center, with two protruding metal tabs out the edges that you had to squeeze together to open it. The stick was preventing the thing from working.

In the mean time, the noises had occasionally resolved them selves into animal noises. Probably cat—evil, possessed, demonic, pissed off cat—but probably cat. I got my tool kit out and started to figure out a way to get the bag open. I could not see a way to do it. The hinges were between the bag and the bike, and I could not dismount the bag or the rack without opening the bag and pulling the pins. If I had the bag open I could easily remove the lock…but…well…back to square-one. Annoying.

I had found a suitable rock that I thought might be able to bash it open (a big rock, these bags were tough) but I really did not want to hurt whatever was in the bag. I was not really a cat person if that's what it was, but it did not ask to be there either. I was not really too happy about whacking on my bike with a rock either. The moron that put it in the bag…now that is something I could cheerfully bash on with a rock. In a last ditch effort to avoid what looked to be massive destruction I decided I would ask the army guys if they had any tools that might help. They had kind-of been looking my way anyway. Apparently they are not used to such strange noises from a machine either. I hate to think what they would have thought if I *had* started bashing my bike with the rock. An exorcism maybe?

Boy did I luck out. These guys were machinists, and were basically a mobile workshop and they really knew their business. After a short and efficient group discussion they whipped out an ungainly looking piece of power equipment that was basically a sideways drill press. They clamped it to the bag frame, and set it to drilling out the hinge pins. Inside of 10 minutes they had the pins removed. Not a scratch, even on the hinge bodies. Only the pins were destroyed. By this time the folks from the RV had joined us, and two other cars had stopped and disgorged onlookers. Twenty-two people were watching as the machinist finished the last pin. He removed his machine and reached for the cover. Twenty-two people had a brief impression of motion as the cover exploded outward and the something small and brown seemed to vanish into the tall grass.

Between all of us we decided it was a kitten. Nobody was really sure. Twenty-one of us went prowling through the grass looking for the poor thing. The twenty-second (lady from the RV) went off to fix us lunch and Kool-aid. We must have been a sight, a bunch of army guys and a few civilians prowling through the grass crying, "Here kitty, kitty, kitty."

About this time a State Trooper zoomed by on the highway. We could hear the tires screeching and see the cloud of dust as he turned around just down the road. I must have looked anxious as the army guy nearest me said with a grin, "Don't worry, we can take 'em out."

The trooper was friendly enough and listened to part of the story before starting to lecture about loitering at a picnic area (uh…what else do you do at a picnic area?).

Anyway he was taken aback by our matronly RV lady that handed him a glass of Kool-aid and a sandwich and said...and I am quoting, "Shut up and eat your sandwich."

Now we were really a sight...a bunch of army guys, a State Trooper, and a few civilians prowling through the grass crying, "Here kitty, kitty, kitty."

Finally the consensus was that we would never find the kitten, but that it was at least better off here, than where it had been. The army guys were packing up to leave. I sidled over and asked one for a little duct tape. He instantly produced a roll of it but asked why.

"I need to tape my side-bag shut."

"Why would you do that?" he asked as he pointed to the bag. The stick was out of the lock and the hinge pins had been replaced with shiny newly made ones. "Your bike's full of gas too, have a safe trip."

Like I said, these guys are good.

Something like an hour later I was approaching Childress. I spotted a police cruiser parked beside the road at the horizon. I let off the gas and glanced at the speedometer. This is the point that nearly ended my motorcycling career, and is as close as I have ever come to getting injured or killed on a motor. You see, there was a furry head poking out the nook between the gauges and the sport fairing. It had large, ungainly ears and large whiskers. It was staring at me with wide, bright-green eyes.

Motorcyclists in general are not easy to surprise. Even exhausted we are on the lookout and alert for unusual things happening on the road and with the traffic around us. Our equipment is intimately familiar to us, and any unusual noise or vibration, no matter how subtle, will bring us instantly alert. This 'hyper-awareness' usually serves us well.

That said, I challenge anyone to have a...uh...less...um...*enthusiastic* reaction than mine.

Trust me. Absolutely nothing can prepare you for a kitten coming out of your speedometer. I am not often given to profanity, but, "Holy Shit!" I think was exactly what I screamed (not yelled, screamed) as I let go of the handlebars and actually nearly climbed off the back of the bike. The bike violently veered across the entire road and back onto the shoulder before I got it back under control and stopped. I hit the kill switch, kicked the stand down, staggered into the grass, and flopped down, trying to get my racing heart and breathing under control.

All these antics of course attracted the attention of the cop, another State Trooper, and he cruised my way. He was not the least impressed by my explanation.

"See for yourself." I said as I pointed to the bike.

There was no kitten to be seen, but this time I knew better. The Trooper carefully peered toward the afore mentioned gap, but due to the glare of the sun, could not see inside. He was still sure I was joshing him so he tapped the speedometer. The reaction was immediate.

Pounce!

Out of the gap flew the kitten, grabbing his finger. The Trooper (Troopers are also very professional and hard to surprise) let out a wild, lengthy girlish scream and was standing 20 yards away in the middle of US 287 with his gun drawn before he regained control of himself. I had hit the dirt when he jumped and the gun appeared, and I was of course crying because I was trying so hard not to laugh. I think he appreciated it, first because he did not shoot me, but also because he let me go after giving me a small blue towel to put in the gap so the kitten would not slide down on top of the hot headlight case. He also gave me a very small teddy bear (what would be called a "beanie baby" now) for the kitten to play with. Troopers carry teddy bears of all sizes and shapes in case they encounter children in stressful situations…and they accept donations if folks are looking for a good cause. Turned out that this was the perfect arrangement. The towel gave the kitten the height to look out when she wished, and she could lie down and sleep when she was bored. Mostly she liked to watch with those big green eyes.

On my next fuel stop when I walked away from the bike, the kitten jumped off and in about two leaps climbed…well…me…and perched on my shoulder. This was to be her custom for the remainder of the time I knew her.

My ever present and crucial deadline told me that I could stop for another meal. A "Kettles" in Denton provided the answer. As I left the bike, "MotoCat" (yeah I named her) assumed her position.

The waitress noticed and asked, "Did you know you have a cat on your shoulder?" Interesting question, that.

"Yep."

"Oh…well…uh…well…um…We can't have a cat in here."

"Okay." I said as I sat down. I was at that moment, 300-pound, hungry, sweaty biker dude. I didn't figure they would throw me out. I was right.

I had been trying to give MotoCat water at every stop. She would not take it. I could only assume that she was not thirsty. Did not know how she could not be, we had been riding in some terrific heat, but again, I was not a cat person.

I ordered a burger and a Dr. Pepper for a change (Cokes were starting to taste bad). MotoCat attacked the Dr. Pepper, lapping it up as fast as she could. She also ate a healthy portion of my burger. I had to order another burger and drink so there would be enough for me.

The waitress evidently decided to have a sense of humor about it all, as she came by the table and asked, "Will that be separate checks?"

To this day I wish I had said, "Yes." Oh well.

The journey was complete. I made the deadline.

The bet: Dallas to Pikes Peak to Dallas on my bike, in under 40 hours.

As I presented the Salt and Pepper shakers to my then roommate and still best-friend he nonchalantly stated, "You're three hours early."

Then with a cocked eyebrow, "Did you know you have a cat on your shoulder?"

The stakes: Well…a Coke. I told you I was a lot younger then. It would take at least a case of Cokes (Diet) to get me to agree to that bet now. Somebody on another bike would have to ride with me also. Also…I am pretty sure he never paid up.

As for MotoCat, she soon was too big for her nook in the fairing. But after I put a leather pad down the center of the tank she would nestle in my lap and dig her front claws into the leather. She loved to ride, and I had to sneak out of the house if I wanted to ride sans cat. We made many miles together until she passed away of leukemia in 1991. She was eight.

And I must admit—now I am a cat person.

Well Oiled

I have always purchased older, 'well-used' motorcycles that have been neglected by their former owners, and fixed them up for my rides. This occasionally leads to 'situations'.

Well, my '80 Yamaha XS-1100 Midnight Special, which I am slowly resurrecting from the previous owner's incompetence, taught me something new today. *Again.*

Southbound on US 75 at 5:30am this morning (at some unmentionable speed…it was beautiful this morning), headed to downtown Dallas for work, I blew an oil cooler line.

Went something like this:

(Blink, Blink) "Why is my vision getting fuzzy?" as a very light spray of oil coated my helmet visor.

(soft pop)

"AwwwwwwwwwwwwwwwSh*ttttOwwwwwwwwwwwwwwwwwGhhh-haaaaaYuckkk!" as a solid stream of hot oil squirts all over me. Elapsed time? I dunno…the speed of thought…maybe a quarter of a second.

Used the engine one more time to get out of the traffic pack (yeah, traffic even sucks at 5:30am here) and hit the kill switch while I was headed for the shoulder. Elapsed time now…three seconds or so. Coasted to a stop (uh…no brakes left…every square inch of the bike, as well as every square inch of me, is covered in oil). Frankly I am praying that the ignition temperature of the oil is substantially higher than the temperature of my pipes. Motorcycle exhaust pipes get quite hot. Pushed the bike off the highway into a parking lot. A quick phone call and the wife came and brought more tools (my tool kit is woefully inadequate). Looped the line and bypassed the cooler circuit. Added oil and drove it home.

Sad thing is, I had the bike apart for fuel and electrical system repairs/upgrades last weekend…which was right after the steering bearing replacement…well used machines need lots of attention.

Anyway, I had eyeballed the oil cooler lines and thought, *Don't look bad, but I think I'll replace 'em.*

Went to the local hydraulic/parts shop and was going to have them make the stainless braided, Teflon-lined lines. They were out of the correct size line and said, "Next weekend".

I said, "Great, no problem." Sigh. That would be tomorrow.

So, my bike has earned her name. She is "Well Oiled Machine." Guess that makes me the "Well Oiled Rider" of the "Well Oiled Machine." *Hmmmmm…*

Summary:

I have discovered a new method for changing the oil. This "revolutionary new automatic, in-flight oil change method" is not highly recommended.

Hot Castroil 15W-40 tastes terrible (and I was wearing a full-face helmet!). Difficult to describe, but it tastes exactly like it smells when you dump a large amount of it on hot pipes. Blech. I can still taste it. I can still smell it for that matter.

An XS oil pump with the engine at 5000+ RPM will pump 3 quarts of oil out a 3/8" id line in about 3 seconds.

There is no point on my XS that is not thoroughly and completely lubricated.

There is no point on me that is not thoroughly and completely lubricated.

I actually have a good-sized burn on my left inside thigh.

The ignition point of Castroil 15W-40 is somewhat higher than the temperature of a fast moving XS's pipes. By how much I do not know. Do not try this at home folks.

When the little voice in your head says "Change the lines", do it right then.

Don't buy used bikes. Yeah I know. I can't follow that one either. But at least keep the former owner's name so when you discover that he used fuel/emission hose (AAAAAAARRRRRGGGGGHHH-HHH!!!) on your high pressure/high temperature oil lines, you can go back and heap abuse on him. I would suggest a lobotomy, but it must be too late. I really feel this was incompetence, bordering on negligence. If you're fixing a bike up to sell, fix it right or leave it alone and sell it broken. Nuff said.

South Padre Island Bike Fest

Motorcycle voyaging is a unique experience. Long trips are often life-changing in subtle ways, despite the apparent mundane nature of the trip. Out there on your own, or with a friend, you learn much about the world and yourself. Doing it on a 20-year old machine can introduce interesting elements too...

PART ONE—OUTBOUND

Alternate Title: *Yyyyyyeeeeeeeeeeaaaaaaaaaaahhhhhhhhh!!!!*
   Alternate Emergency Backup Title: *Texas is a Bloody Big State!*
   Title if News Headline: *Massive Oil Spill Covers South-Central Texas—Trail Leads to Local Man.*
   Well the time had finally arrived. The South Padre Island Bike Fest was here. Time for my best friend James and I to saddle up our 20+ year old machines and leave for the 1000-mile round-trip journey from Dallas to South Texas. With side trips, back-roads, and sightseeing we fully expected to ride 1100–1200 miles on this trip. We underestimated that by nearly 50% (we always do), but more on that later.
   Unfortunately due to an incompetent tugboat driver, the Queen Isabelle Causeway Bridge was knocked down in mid-September. This is the only route onto South Padre Island, and will not be repaired until the end of December, so the Bike Fest, otherwise known as "Roar by the Shore" was moved to Harlingen…a few miles inland. Bummer. No beach. We briefly considered canceling the trip, but frankly with the accumulated stress of our jobs and life in general, they could have held the Bike Fest on an oilrig in the middle of the gulf, and it would

have been preferable to staying home. We'd have found a way to ride there too!

A couple of disclaimers are necessary here:

First and foremost as far as disclaimers go, is that anything a law enforcement professional might construe as evidence of an illegal act on our parts—particularly traffic violations—is to be considered fiction…nay…a complete figment of imagination. I do not even exist…so obviously I could not have gone say…135 mph at any time on this ride. Stealth bike personified. So to paraphrase the fiction writers—who often write more truth than fiction anyway, "Any similarities to any person living or dead—especially to those two living persons that took this ride—or to places or roads these events are set in is strictly unintentional". So there.

You will find a bunch of unsolicited advice and some product endorsements contained herein. Take them with a grain of salt. Your mileage may vary. I am not selling anything however, and have no vested interest in anything I mention (but if you want to send me $19.95 I will send you…something…maybe out of my garage…possibly worth…something…).

The "Great Pepsi Conspiracy" also becomes evident in the below paragraphs. Something has to be done…really…It may already be too late, and that would be a terrible thing, as if it is already too late, then we are all well and truly doomed.

There is also some of the *us* vs. *them* stuff in here. This is the usually friendly ribbing and other shenanigans that go on between the "Rice Burners" and the Harleys. Before you fire off an angry letter to me about it, please note that I do believe, and have always believed that if you ride, you are a rider, no matter what you are astride. There is no animosity intended or felt about this issue, just the good-natured ribbing between riders. I can recognize the merits of a well-maintained machine and appreciate and admire the work that has gone into one even if it is not a machine that I would select for myself. The world would be pretty boring if we were all alike (we are getting very close guys and gals, be careful). And for the record, I do wave to all other riders, and proudly ride a Rice Burner (a Japanese make bike).

Background:
I ride a 1980 Yamaha XS-1100 "Midnight Special". These are fairly rare machines, and during their era were the fastest production cruiser made. They earned a reputation for speed, reliability, and sheer "yee-ha" factor that has yet to be surpassed by a cruiser. Some of the "crotch rocket" or sport type bike types can out run her (we also refer to those as "zip-splats"), but you would be permanently folded into pretzel shape if you attempted to ride a "zip-splat" more than 50 miles in a stretch.

All my complex constructions have names (and personalities), and this bike is no exception. She is "Well Oiled Machine" and, as explained in the story *Well Oiled*, she really did earn that name. She confirmed her name in spades on this trip, but more about that later.

I rescued "Well Oiled Machine" in August 2000 from a completely incompetent former owner. She was in a sad state of neglect, but ran like a demon, and I have spent the last year fixing and improving her. There is still more to do—there always is—but she looks and rides like a champ. She recently got her faded and chipped gold chrome redone in real chrome, and new custom polyurethane gloss black tank paint. The wheels have also been redone in black. She is looking really sharp.

Maybe this statement will explain how well this bike rides, and how much I like her—although I may buy a new bike someday (I am really eyeing those Valkyries), that would probably be an additional bike. I would not trade "Well Oiled Machine" for a new bike even if it were an even swap.

The other rider on this trip was James. James is my best friend, and one of the few people I would trust with my life. James rides a 1981 GL-1100 Gold Wing. This bike was purchased for a ridiculously low sum after having been stored for 15 years. "Bunnie", (don't ask) has only 10,000 original miles and is in immaculate shape after he took care of a few minor mechanical issues caused by the long-term storage. James has been my best friend for longer than either of us care to remember (something over 21 years at last count). We have been riding together much of that time and are extremely compatible in our riding styles. On a long trip it is important that team riders prefer the same speeds, distances between breaks, and riding styles. We have been doing it for so long, and are so similar in styles that we are almost psychic as a pair. James usually leads.

We're Outta Here...

On Tuesday October 9th we were ready. The bikes were loaded, clean, packed, and as mechanically sound as we could make them. Every thing was ready. We departed Dallas about 10:30am into threatening weather and headed for Kerrville. By the direct route, Kerrville splits the difference between Dallas and Brownsville, and James's grandfather lives there. Looked like a great place to layover, splitting the 500-mile ride roughly in half and placing our arrival for Wednesday just after the rally check–in opens. Of course we were not taking the direct route, we rarely do—where is the fun in that? Interstate 35 out of Dallas is the direct route, and is a terrible way to go. Packed with trucks, truck tire carcasses (road gators), horribly inept car-drivers, and construction—and decidedly lacking in scenery—Interstate 35 is both absolutely boring and marginally unsafe for the touring motorcyclist.

We were on vacation, and the schedule was not critical. A few miles out of the way for the scenic back roads can't hurt. We both work under constant and very difficult deadlines. Why transfer that to our time off? Time for the vacation attitude to kick in.

Riding is the point...yes?

We hooked a right out of Dallas on US 67 and zoomed toward Stephenville. We were headed for a cut-off about 20 miles short of Stephenville that would take us onto US 281, which headed more or less in the direction we wanted to go. Actually, US 281 goes exactly where we wanted to go—if you stay on it forever it ends in Browns-ville—but it jams through San Antonio and then joins with Interstate 37 for a while, so it just did not quite take the route we wanted. Our first fuel stop was to be Hico, which sits on the junction of the cut-off and US 281. This was just at a 100-mile leg of the trip. I was leading out of Dallas, though our usual configuration is for James to lead.

The sky was very threatening, and getting worse, which actually made for a beautiful ride. As we got further away from Dallas the landscape opened up and revealed an interesting vista when combined with the blues and blacks and occasional startlingly golden sunbeams penetrating the mountainous sky. The fantastic lightning displays in the distance promised an interesting day to come, but were nonetheless beautiful. As the traffic eased and the speeds climbed I could feel the tensions of the past few weeks melting away. If everybody rode motorcycles on occasion, the therapists would be out of business. Every five minutes or so I found myself wanting to yell out in sheer joy. That is that "yee-ha" factor I was referring to earlier.

If you like music, I have the secret weapon for long distance motorcycle riding. I love and must have music, and having good music while riding is an additional thrill and source of almost constant joy. It makes the miles roll by, and makes every new minute a sheer pleasure. The secret weapon is mp3's. There are a variety of portable ways to play mp3 files. I have a Walkman-like portable CD player that will accept CD's that have mp3 files burned onto them. I took all my CD's, 200 or so, and ripped the songs I love to mp3's on my computer. I then burned these files onto a couple of new CDs. One CD will hold about 10 hours of music! My player has what I refer to as "descending random order" where it will play songs randomly, but will not play the same song twice. Start it up and you will be surprised how fast the miles go by.

You catch yourself saying (right after you yell out in sheer joy), "Damn good music they're playing…here comes another one…man, I love that song!" You *must* watch your speed under these conditions…it climbs all by itself.

Good riding. Good music. Good friend. Sheer Heaven.

US 67 runs more west than south, and the winds were quite fierce out of the south, so we were dealing with substantial crosswinds. During one particularly strong episode an 18-wheeler passed going the opposite direction. The "whoosh" was so intense it sucked open the one-gallon Ziploc bag that is kept Velcro-ed to my instrument panel and tucked into the nook the sport-fairing creates. The contents—a map, extra CD, and miscellaneous instructions—came loose inside the fairing. I actually managed to corral them all and stuff them back into the bag, all the while somehow managing to keep the bike on an even track. Some crosswinds. Behind me James was playing with his Gold Wing. He was apparently seeing how far he could lean into the crosswind and stay in a straight line. The results were impressive!

Soon the rain began to spatter down, and the sky grew even more ominous. The forecast, if you put any stock at all in those things, was calling for "a chance" of "scattered widespread rain" over the entire state. *Huh?* Scattered, widespread rain. Humph. Seems like a safe forecast to make, as it makes no sense at all and cannot possibly give anybody any meaningful information. Weather guys would make good politicians.

As the sky in front of us got even worse and the rain began to come down heavier we pulled over to don our rain-gear. Looked like we would spend the majority of this trip in the water and fighting headwinds. Oh well. Beats working. We had about 50 miles to go to Hico, and as we took off again James took the lead.

I will digress a bit and talk about team riding. When a pair of motorcyclists is headed some place, they must agree on who is leading at any given time. Generally the leader will ride the left side of the lane, and the follower, or chase, will ride the right side of the lane, a couple of bike lengths back. There are several variations of this, some of which are hotly debated, but in general this makes you more visible to cars. This protects your lane and road-space from the unsafe or inconsiderate auto driver that for some reason has decided you do not need or do not deserve your entire lane, while providing room for both motorcycles to maneuver should something happen. The leader sets the pace, initiates lane changes, passing, stops, and navigation. The chase's job is to stay with the leader, anticipate his movements and help reserve traffic space, and most importantly, to not run into the leader Seems obvious doesn't it? If not equipped with two-way radios, the chase will pass the leader and pull off or take the lead if information needs to be exchanged.

A long-distance team or group ride needs to consist of riders with similar skill levels, endurance, and riding styles, or the trip can become hell to everyone involved. As mentioned above, James and I have been riding together for years, and we are as good as a team as we are individually. We are so matched in riding skills and styles that we are almost psychic concerning what the other is up to. For instance, when I am chase and really need a break, about the time that I consider passing James and pulling off, he will pull off somewhere of his own accord. Also, when chase, if I spot a traffic situation ahead of James, I know exactly what he is going to do and when he is going to do it, and I can act/react accordingly. The same goes if I am the lead. I need to know what the person behind me will do, so I am free to maneuver as needed. It takes time, practice, mistakes, trust, and many, many miles to develop this ability. James and I are at its pinnacle and find as much pleasure riding together as a team as we do cooking down an empty highway individually.

Back to the road and the rain. Motorcyclists generally avoid wearing raingear if possible as the gear is somewhat hot, stuffy, and clammy. Very shortly our decision to don the raingear was warranted when we truly got into a heavy downpour. James and I have had a lot of adverse weather experience, and shortly, 70 mph and twenty–foot rooster tails demonstrated that motorcycles are indeed stable in the rain. Thankfully our 20+ year old ignition systems were still impervious to water. Yuck. Puddles, spray, and road film. So much for the bikes being clean.

After we got moving, a softball sized clump of clay-like substance about the size of a horse-apple flew off an oncoming 18-wheeler and thumped me in the meat of my left leg, just below the knee. The impact was staggering. Let's see, 70 mph (my velocity) plus 70 mph (the trucks velocity) plus a couple pounds of flying object adds up to um…well…pain. Ouch. I still sport the bruise.

Twenty or so miles of heavy rain, and we made the cut-off for Hico. The rain suddenly left us, and the rest of the way to Hico was dry. We stopped at a convenience store to gas up. While gassing up I noted several heavy drops of something on my left boot. Since I was still smarting from the substantial whack I received on the leg, I stooped to wipe a couple of drops off, basically to see if it was blood. Turned out to be oil, which was probably worse. I checked the oil in the bike, and it was not low. There was a small amount of oil on the front center of the engine, just below the cam-chain tensioner. Since a minor leak at this tensioner is a common "bug" on these bikes, and I could spot no other problem, I made a mental note to keep an eye on it, and we continued on. I did point it out to James, so he would be aware of the situation.

As we gassed up the bikes, we looked to the south. It looked like extremely heavy rain was rapidly moving into our route. Lightning, thunder, and high winds were obviously prominent features of this storm. James looked over and said, "Think we should try to run it?" He was suggesting that we could push on, hard and fast, to try to beat or get ahead of the storm.

I thought briefly about it. The hell with it. We are on vacation. "Nah. Let's get some lunch." I could tell that I gave the expected and agreeable answer.

Like I said, almost psychic.

Hico is an interesting town. Typical small town Texas I think. No chain restaurants, except the ever-present McDonalds and Dairy Queen. They do have "Major Brand Gas". Really…the station is actually called "Major Brand Gas". In a town like this, if you want a good meal, ask somebody where to go. They will be happy to tell you.

I stepped inside the convenience store and asked the clerk, "Where is a good place to get some lunch?"

I could tell she was sizing me up. She said somewhat warily, "About all we've got around here is barbeque and a family style place, and you're a-bit late for lunch at the family style place." 300-pound guys in leather frequently have that effect. Wears off quickly though.

"Well that's great, I am in the mood for some good barbeque anyway." I am always on the lookout for good barbeque.

Her eyes immediately lit up. "Well then hon, just take a right, right there," she chuckled as she waved vaguely toward the south side of the store, "and hang a left on the first street. He's right there. Can't miss him."

I could tell that if that was not enough information for me to find it, then I surely did not deserve it.

I came out of the store and mounted up. James was just finishing his cigar. "Barbeque or family style?" I asked, already knowing the answer.

"Barbeque."

"Perfect."

We found the place with no trouble, a converted house in a residential neighborhood. No inside seating, just picnic tables set right next to the pits, outside under a tin roof. It was deserted.

We parked the bikes, removed our riding gear, and stepped inside. An older gentleman greeted us. "You boys hungry?"

"Yes sir," and "Absolutely," were our honest replies.

"Well, you are a bit late for lunch, but I'll fix you up," he said as we stepped back outside. "I've got some sausage and some smoked pork patties left," he stated as he opened the nearest pit.

I've never had smoked pork patties, brisket done right is my idea of barbeque, but he seemed to be suggesting it and they looked good (they were huge and I was hungry), so that's what I chose. James followed suite.

As he constructed our plates he made idle conversation, "I'd offer brisket, but it won't be ready until dinner. The lunch crowd ate a bunch today." Another characteristic of a small Texas town. Lunch in Dallas is anywhere between 9am and midnight, depending on what you are up to. Lunch in a small town is...well...lunch.

He presented us with plates full of potato salad, coleslaw, baked barbeque beans, and sides of pickle and onion (not for James, he cannot stand onions). Some bread and barbeque sauce finished filling the plates, and a couple of Diet Cokes topped off the meal (Diet Coke was notoriously hard to get on this trip due to the Great Pepsi Conspiracy—a fact we did not fully appreciate until later). The patties were excellent. They were at least a pound and were basically a smoked hamburger. Wow. A real ham, hamburger. How about that? Very different. Very tasty. Good place. I need to come back sometime during the lunch crowd. I have to try his brisket.

After a leisurely (and tasty) lunch we got ready to go again. As we pulled out of town we were really glad that we had chosen to stop for lunch, rather than attempt to beat the storm. For the next 100 or so miles everywhere we were, was where the storm had just been. We had to deal with large puddles and very wet roads, but there was no rain. Had we been about 30 minutes or an hour ahead of ourselves we would have been in the midst of the storm the entire way. We could tell by the water on and beside the road that it had been a serious storm. Wind-blown debris scattered about reinforced the impression. There are more benefits to the "vacation attitude" than advertised.

The "comfortable" fuel range on my bike is 100 miles. This is generally the maximum distance I plan between fuel stops. I generally hit reserve at just about 108 miles, and the reserve on my bike won't take me much further (maybe 15 miles). I could go further if I drove very conservatively, but "Well Oiled Machine" just will not go 65 mph. *Must* go faster. This is compatible with James' bike, as although his cruiser holds more fuel, due to some remaining complications associated with the long-term storage, his reserve function is out of commission. He could go further than I can, but if he runs out, he has to push. Not fun, as one of the prime rules of the Universe is that if you have to push a bike, it is inevitably always uphill.

For me, an overriding factor to the fuel range comes into play, and that is the fact that after 100 miles, I am ready to get off the machine and take a break. Gas stops give you the needed excuse. Two more stops would be needed today, although one was only miles from our destination.

We spun off of US 281 on Texas 29 to Llano. At Llano we would catch Texas 16 to Kerrville. Llano is the beginnings of the hill country, and is an example of how diverse Texas really is. In Texas, you can drive through desert, pine forests, mountains, salt flats, beaches, and swamps. You can get a thousand miles away from home without leaving the state. Llano is wine country. Vineyards abound in the area, and the roads promised more scenery than the other possible routes to Kerrville. As we gassed up in Llano I silently showed James the rather large amount of oil all over my left boot. The bike was still not low on oil, so I did not have to worry about the engine, but it was obvious the problem was getting worse. We took off, and the rain was pretty much gone, so we had a pleasant ride into Kerrville.

We arrived at James' grandfather's (Si's) place shortly before dusk. Si has a beautiful place, all built with his own hands, overlooking the Texas hill country. The house and several large workshops and such were hand constructed out of the native stone and hardwoods. The house is nothing short of spectacular with a huge stone and iron fireplace and beam supported vaulted ceiling being the central features of the living room. Si is a character, and I hope I am in his physical and mental condition when I reach those years. He is strong, and still works in stone and wood—hand-crafting furniture not just from cut lumber—but he starts with the trees and makes his own cut lumber!

Si arrived home from a grocery run shortly after we got there, and we piled into his Ford pickup and zipped into town to eat. James and I loaded up on delicious fried catfish with all the trimmings while Si teased the waitress. Guys, when you get to be an old man, one immediately noted benefit is that you can say things to the waitresses that a younger man would get arrested for. The unsuspecting younger men that are with you will also probably choke and snort iced tea out of their nostrils when they hear some of the things you are getting away with, and I am sure that holds high entertainment value. For the first time I am looking forward to one aspect of getting older.

After we arrived back at Si's place we pulled my bike into the shop and examined it closer for the source of the oil leak. Due to the distribution of the oil on the front of the engine it was readily apparent that the leak was at the cam tensioner. Looking closely we found that the rubber plug in the end of it was missing, so we fabricated and installed a new plug. Si can construct anything in his shop, with supplies on hand. The new plug should take care of the problem, as the oil leaking at the cam tensioner is not under pressure. It is just return oil and oil mist in the crankcase. Again, this is a known "bug" with these bikes, and is not a major issue. We ran the bike and gave it a once over. Everything seemed in order, and there was no new oil to be seen.

I looked in disgust at my machine. She had been sparklingly clean in Dallas, but now several hundred miles of road film and leaking oil had taken its toll. There was a baked on gook all along her left side exhaust pipe, completely obscuring the chrome with what looked like the stuff that accumulates in the bottom of an oven...when a guy is doing the cooking! Yuck. Oil was everywhere. As I gave "Well Oiled Machine" a final glance before turning in for the night, I noted the oil and gunk everywhere. I also noted my well oiled left-boot, and the oil that had soaked my jeans up my leg to the knee. I commented softly, "Glad we got this fixed, you're making me feel like I'm riding a Harley."

Guys, listen carefully...

Never...never...never......*ever*...insult a woman. Even if she deserves it.

PART TWO—BREAKDOWN

I showered and was asleep before my head hit the pillow. Zonk. I was completely oblivious to anything until I smelled breakfast. Long distance riding, and the Texas hill-country quiet and fresh air are apparently good for sleep and the appetite.

Si had a huge pile of scrambled eggs, a frying pan full of homemade venison/pork smoked sausage, a stack of buttered toast, and several varieties of homemade jams ready and waiting. James and I provided ourselves with our requisite morning caffeine fix with the Diet Cokes we had (with remarkable foresight) grabbed at our last gas stop the night before. We devoured it all in short order, thanked Si profusely for his hospitality, and prepared to pull out.

An unrecognized but fortunate premonition caused me to pull on my favorite riding jeans. These jeans are a pair of heavy denim jeans that happen to fit me best out of all that I currently own. See, I have been seriously dieting (yet eating bunches of foods like described above) and have lost a lot of weight. As a result most of my pants no longer fit, being several sizes too large. What a problem to have. Anyway my current favorite jeans were the ones that fit the best, and were also not so coincidentally the oil-soaked pair that I had ridden in yesterday.

We pulled out of Si's place and stopped at the nearby convenience store to grab another Diet Coke and to top off the gas. Neither James nor I is worth much in the morning until we get our minimum dose of caffeine. For me it is usually delivered via iced tea, but Diet Coke can suffice in a pinch. For James it is Diet Coke. No substitutions allowed.

I also checked my oil and given the mess, was not surprised to find it low. There was no new oil on my boot, and none dripping off the bike, so I was confident that the replacement plug had fixed the problem. The oil level in most machines is checked via a sight glass located low in the crankcase. Mine is no exception. I purchased a couple quarts and began to top it off. At first I could clearly see the oil running by the glass, and added a quart. I thought the oil had still not reached the line so I added another one. When I poured the third one in I knew something was wrong, The bike only holds about 4 quarts. Out comes the flashlight, and we determined that in my willingness to believe I had lost a lot of oil, I had overfilled it—probably by about two quarts. This is not wise, but I am familiar with the workings of this engine and knew that it would not do any harm. I admit it only because I know that every other motorcyclist has done the same at one time or another. Don't bother denying it.

We left Kerrville via Texas 173 headed south. This road kind of hooks around San Antonio and then connects with Texas 16 again. We wound through several back roads, finding our way through the town of "Free" and also drove through "San Diego". *Hmmm.* When did California become part of Texas? One sign of note somewhere along this route read "Fried Chicken Maps Available". I wanted one of those maps.

During this ride I became aware that oil was again streaming off the front of my engine and all over my left boot and leg. It was now apparent that the leak was only evident either at high rpm's or when the bike was hot. It was also much worse than it had been. I motioned to James and we stopped for a break. Again, I could not find the source of the oil. I could only figure that it had to be the gasket between the cylinder jugs and the crankcase. It could not possibly be pressure oil, as it would leak much more rapidly, and be very visible. A check of the oil lines that are on the back of the engine confirmed that they were intact, and there was no evidence of leakage around them.

I was still overfull of oil, so I rationalized that it must be a gasket as we had conjectured earlier, and that the overfilling had just exaggerated the leak. It would return to its earlier volume as the oil got closer to its normal level. Nothing to do about it here anyway. Time to press on.

Our purpose for meandering around the several back-roads was to again reach US 281 south of where it splits back off of Interstate 37. US 281 is one of only a couple of routes to Brownsville. We reached

US 281 at Alice, and looked around for somewhere to eat some lunch. Nothing obvious presented itself. We apparently blinked and completely missed Alice, and we had enough gas to make the additional 25 miles to the town of Falfurrias, so we headed there.

About halfway there, a state trooper went by fast in the other direction. In my mirror I caught a glimpse of him scattering dust and gravel turning around in the median (dangerous to other traffic and illegal). We were not really speeding…something around 73–75 in a 70 zone, but state troopers are famous for driving at high speeds and coming up behind unsuspecting drivers. They would also write their own mother a ticket for 2 miles over the limit, so it is well to be wary of them. I was unsure if James had seen the trooper turn around or not, so I pulled up beside him and motioned to "take it easy". He waved me into the lead, and we pulled into Falfurrias a few minutes later. The trooper was not seen again. Maybe he got stuck in the median. One can only hope.

We were low on fuel, but I needed a break more than gas so I pulled off into the shade of a tree in the parking lot of a Dairy Queen on the outskirts of town. Before I had even gotten my helmet off, James pointed down. Oil was streaming off my bike in large quantities. The pipes were beginning to smoke. At the same instant I had that uniquely male…well…feeling that the oil, by now all over both legs, had seeped up my legs far enough to reach a somewhat…sensitive…area. This was bad. Castroil 20W50 is not suitable body oil. Oil was also all over James' windshield, just from that short stint of my leading. Something had to be done.

The bike was really still too hot to examine, so after checking the oil—amazingly it was still not low, although it was now in the normal range—we elected to cruise into town and find a restaurant where we could get a good meal. We would eat, the bike would cool enough for a thorough examination, and we could then decide what to do, depending on what exactly the problem was.

As we drove through town it was obvious that whatever it was, it had really cut loose now. Oil was running off the engine and onto the pipes in great quantities. Crap. I started to worry about bursting into flames, as motorcycle pipes get quite hot. It is mildly embarrassing to sit at a stoplight engulfed in a cloud of your own smoke. Only Harley riders ever get used to it (ducking for cover!)

We pulled into a restaurant/hotel combination at the south end of town.

"Drinks?" the waitress asked.

"Diet Coke." we both said.

"Pepsi ok?" she asked sweetly. Uh Oh. The Pepsi Conspiracy starts.

"No. Thank you. No. Uh. No.

"Tea for me please." I said, feeling pretty safe. In Texas you are legally allowed to burn down any restaurant that serves bad iced tea. James ordered the same. He has to be truly desperate to drink Diet Pepsi.

We then proceeded to have the worst chicken fried steak in the state of Texas. I kept taking another bite, incredulous that it could be that bad and expecting it to get better. I finished the entire thing in that manner. I did not think it was possible to get a bad chicken-fried in Texas. I mean, all you have to do is deep fry some miscellaneous cut of meat and douse it in gravy. How can you screw that up? Last I heard it was still a hanging offense. Texans can expertly fry a chicken-fried, barbeque, and make good iced tea just minutes out of their mother's womb. This can be somewhat disconcerting to the many soon-to-be mothers that have moved here from another state and are giving birth to their first Texan. Having your newborn demand a deep-fryer and barbeque pit instead of crying when the doctor gives them that first "whack" generally causes at least a lifted eyebrow to a non-Texan.

The owner or manager loudly argued and berated the staff the entire time we were in there, resulting in a very unpleasant meal. This on top of my mood induced by being doused in several quarts of hot Castroil, as well as the uncertainty of our situation made for an ugly mood. In silence I paid the check and we walked out to the bikes.

I checked the oil and it was off the sight glass. I had lost at least a quart on the short jaunt through town. I added the quart I had in reserve in my saddle-bag—a little premonition again. I then started the engine, and watched while it pumped the quart of oil out in a matter of about a minute.

This was infuriating! I still could not see exactly where it was coming from! It was pooling on the front of the engine, along the fin just below where the cylinder jugs meet the crankcase. Best as I could tell it was leaking from there. Time was running out too, Five o'clock was approaching and we could tell that most of the town would roll up shortly.

I was envisioning having to summon a trailer from Dallas, several hundred miles away. I could see my vacation ruined...and James' along with it, and was formulating plans to somehow get hold of another bike and get back to the rally before the weekend when the bulk of activities occurred. *Sheesh*, we already had rooms paid for in Brownsville. This would be a tight, hard, few days—with getting my bike back to Dallas and somehow getting back to Brownsville. The idea of abandoning "Well Oiled Machine" entirely even presented itself.

I have a rule with vehicles. If they strand you, they are history, unless the breakdown is the result of your own bumbling or incompetence. By my rule, they are allowed to breakdown or have problems, but they must get you home, or be repairable on the road with what you can scrounge on hand. "Well Oiled Machine" had already stranded me once in rather spectacular fashion and thus earned her name (see *Well Oiled*). I forgave her that incident as she was new to me and I was still fixing things that the former owner had screwed up. That breakdown was the direct result of the former owner's messing about.

Another stranding looked imminent, and that would mean she would have to go. Machines all have personalities, and if yours strands you, it does not like you. Get rid of it. This was beginning to sadden me, as this bike is nimble, comfortable, and powerful and I really enjoy riding her. She can run circles around most other machines, and looks good doing it.

"We may have to rename her 'The Exxon Valdez'." said James with a grin.

I chuckled. "Yeah. At least we won't get lost." I said as I waved at the trail of oil leading out of the parking lot and up the street. We could probably follow it home.

My mood dropped again. Shit. I didn't want to abandon my bike. Neither did I want to spend the night here, and possibly have to endure a breakfast at this place.

I spoke to James, "Go find an auto parts store and get some oil, and maybe some JB weld." I was still thinking gasket, and if I could find it, I could plug it. Oil on the front of the engine could *not* be pressure oil. If this did not work, I would be stuck here. We would not get another chance today, it was getting late and the town was about to close down. *That* would bode ill for "Well Oiled Machine". I was staring intently at her, and my mood was black.

A barely audible feminine voice intruded into my thoughts, *"Wait..."* said 'Well Oiled Machine' quietly. She had gone too far and was starting to realize it.

James was gearing up to go on the oil run. Anything I needed, I had to know about *now*.

I spoke to 'Well Oiled Machine' clearly and deliberately. Those that know me do not find this the least bit unusual, "Listen carefully. If you strand me, you are history. I'll haul your ass back to Dallas and sell you piece by piece on Ebay." As if that was not enough I carefully added, "Then I'll buy a Harley."

That did it. *"Try again,"* she said quietly. There was a certain amount of contriteness. Just enough. Barely. I am a guy, she is a gal. That was all I was going to get.

"Hang on James. Let me check her again."

I started her up and watched intently as a truly massive amount of oil streamed off the front of the engine. At least a quart in 30 seconds. I shut her down and crossed my arms. Sheesh.

"What do you think?" asked James, knowing full well I would have the answer shortly. I am good with machines, and he probably overhead the comment about Ebay and Harley.

I looked again at the pressure oil lines on the back of the engine. They are braided stainless, Teflon lined premium line. They should easily outlast the bike. They and their terminating fittings were clearly visible, and very little oil was present anywhere back there. That was remarkable in itself given the state of the rest of the bike, and certainly indicated that there could not be a leak here.

I rounded on James, "Man this *has* to be pressure oil. There is no damn way that much oil could leak from a small breach in a return path. If this were a gasket, we would find it sticking out of the engine! Shit, I should be able to stick my finger in a hole that could leak that much."

James nodded. He is used to being my sounding board, and would take no offense at either language or tone. "Gotta be the lines then."

"Yep," I agreed, "but I can't see it…let me have your Leatherman's tool."

For those that do not know, a Leatherman's tool is a wonderful stainless gadget that is combination screwdriver, knife, pliers, and about 60 other tools. You could do heart surgery with only that if the need arose. In the movie *Six Days, Seven Nights* Ann Heche says to Harrison Ford, "You're one of those *guy* guys aren't you…you know…one of those guys that could go out into the wilderness with nothing but a Q-tip and build a shopping mall?" Harrison Ford has to answer "no"…but if he had a Leatherman's tool…

Anyway, James passed me the tool. I extended the needle-nose portion and reached in under the tank to push on the top fitting of the oil line. It moved!

"Well damn!" says I. "The fitting is loose. The oil must be wicking along a cooling fin or something to the front of the engine." I did not think that would have been possible with that volume of oil, but there it was.

"Cool. Pull your seat and tank and let's get it fixed."

"Yeah. Go for the oil though. We're going to need it." I said while rapidly thinking. "Grab a roll of those blue paper shop towels and a can of engine degreaser too."

"Anything else?" he said with a raised eyebrow.

"Yeah…a Diet Coke!"

About this time the restaurant owner walked by. "One of those is losing some oil."

Because of my ultra supreme self-control, I resisted a smart-assed comment and basically told him we knew what the problem was and would be out of the way shortly.

"Sorry about the mess." I said as I waved at the ever expanding and impressively large puddle of oil.

"No problem!" he said. "I don't care what you do. I just sold this place and the Hotel too!"

Hmmm. Maybe that explains the bad chicken-fried.

By the time James got back from the supply run, I had moved the bike into the shade of a tree across the parking lot, spread out the tool kit, and had the bags, seat, and tank off. An unfortunate fact of motorcycles is that you usually have to take practically the entire thing apart to work on any given part of it. Step one to change a headlight is probably to remove the rear tire.

I had a good news, bad news, good news kind of thing. The good news was that it definitely was the fitting leaking. The bad news was that it was not loose, it was broken. The good news was that we had a few minutes left before 5pm. We had to move fast.

"Go back to the store and get me a 17 millimeter wrench. I cannot get this fitting loose with the Crescent wrench." Damn thing just wouldn't quite grab it. "Find out who makes hydraulic lines!"

If a town is big enough to have an auto-parts store, there is always a shop that makes hydraulic lines around. I set to work on removing the other end of the line from the oil cooler. I would have to take the entire line to the shop and have a new fitting crimped on.

James returned with the wrenches, and I removed the broken fitting in about 30 seconds. The right tools can really make a difference. I already had the rest of the line off.

He tossed me his bike keys as he relayed the good news, "Napa about two blocks up and on the left makes the lines. Hurry, they close in a few minutes."

I headed for the Napa. Good news, bad news again. Yes they make hydraulic lines, but they have never seen a banjo fitting that size before.

"Help me out guys…there has to be something…" Texans do not give up easily.

"Go see the auto-works guy out by Bob's old dairy. He is a pretty good welder. Maybe he can braise it." suggested the older guy.

"Thanks. I will. But I don't know where the old dairy is."

"Oh, that's over where the big red barn used to be." chimed in the other clerk helpfully.

Finally they realized I was not from there. "North two lights, then left. On the left past the water-tower, just outside of town." said the older guy.

"Great! Thanks!" I yelled as I was already out the door. It was 4:58pm.

The welder looked skeptical. "Might not work, might damage the line from the heat."

"Well I am already stranded, you can't make it worse. The line is Teflon, so it will not melt if we work fast."

He nodded, then proceeded to expertly and quickly braise the fitting back together. He then pressure tested it and pronounced it as good as it could be, "Probably better than when it was new…the tubing part is copper…you never use copper tubing on something that vibrates as much as a motorcycle, vibration work hardens it until it gets brittle."

Good enough. I'll rip the entire thing off and replace it when I get back to Dallas. The bill was five bucks. As I drove away he said, "Come back if you still have trouble, I'll be here!"

Neat town.

It took about 5 minutes to put the oil line back on, then another 20 minutes to install the tank, seat, soft saddlebags, and the two seat bags I was carrying. I pulled the bike around to the back of the hotel and drenched it with two full cans of engine degreaser. After sitting for about 5 minutes, I hosed it off using the hotel's water hose. The degreaser pretty thoroughly cleaned most of the bike, although it did not even touch the baked on gook on the pipes. I stooped down and tried to scratch some of the stuff off with a fingernail. Not a chance.

I looked up at James and raised an eyebrow.

"Yuck." he said.

"I'll never get this crap off right now. Let's ride."

A quick stop for gas, and we were gone. Wish I could say the same for the chicken-fried steak. It was with me for another 100 miles.

It was good to be on the road again. "Well Oiled Machine" was running smooth, and not leaking so much as a trace of oil. The tunes were good, and my mood immediately lightened. The speeds climbed as we headed south.

I have to say, this stretch of US 281 is nearly the most boring road I have ever driven. Straight, flat and level as far as the eye can see. Only some scrub Mesquite trees and plains grasses barely hang on here. It got so bad that we were intentionally getting as close to the plentiful "road gators" as we could without hitting them (well...mostly) just to have something to do. If you locked your throttle, put your feet up on the handlebars, and went to sleep you would stand an even chance of reaching your destination. There is nothing out here. I know from experience that the only road worse, is US 77 running between Kingsville and Brownsville. These are basically the only two roads in this part of Texas that go this way.

Now dark, we pressed on. Now we really had something to do, spotting the "road gators" in time to swerve around them. In Edinburg we hit Texas 107 and headed to Harlingen. We got to drive through such towns as La Blanca (She's white? White Girl?), Elsa, and James' favorite—Ed Couch.

We reached Harlingen, checked in at the Bike Fest (at the dog racing track), and headed for our accommodations in Brownsville.

After we checked in at the hotel, we wanted nothing more than to sleep. Briefly thought about it, but it turns out both our stomachs were making demands. We were hungry. Make that *hungry*. Apparently our bellies were insisting that we cover up that bad chicken-fried with something. Maybe anything.

We decided that after we both showered and donned clean clothes we would find something to eat. In my room, it got interesting when I had to cut my left boot off with a pocketknife. Even though the uppers were leather, the oil had sought out and found parts of the tongue, lacing and lacing reinforcement that were synthetic and chemically welded them all together. I dumped the oil out of my boot, and was still thinking I could save them, when I noticed the serious rash and swelling on the front part of my ankle and the top of my foot. A less obvious but much itchier rash was all over the rest of my leg and up to some sensitive areas. I upended the boot again and even more oil dripped out. I tossed the boots, socks, and underwear in the trash. I do not recommend Castroil as a skin-oil.

A long hot shower, and a complete bar of hotel soap and bottle of hotel shampoo later I had all the oil off of me. I felt alive again. I bagged the jeans so they would not drip oil on the hotel furnishings and went to find James. It was dinnertime.

PART THREE—THE RALLY

The next thing I remember is waking up in the morning. I have a credit card receipt from Wednesday night from IHOP in my wallet, so I assume we ate something there. About 20 bucks worth.

The rally did not have much scheduled for Thursday. Our intention was to clean up the bikes, and maybe visit the vendor's area. In short, we were not going to strain ourselves today.

I gave the bagged oily jeans to the hotel laundry with instructions to wash them hard, but *not* to wash them with anything else. I almost laughed at the guy when he told me that they were jeans, and washing them with other things would not hurt them. I did not repeat myself, I do not give instructions for services I am paying for, just to have fun.

I was just hoping to get a pair of work-jeans back. The wife and I are rebuilding a 20-ton steel sailboat in our spare time, and work clothes are needed in plentiful supply.

James and I headed to the IHOP for a large breakfast. Something with pancakes I believe. Afterward we headed to find a car wash, with a side trip to grab a couple Diet Cokes and for James to replenish his cigar supply.

A note of amusement: James spent the entire rest of the trip buying out the cigar supply at every store and gas station we stopped at. Seems his brand is not popular around these parts, and nobody had more than one or two packages.

At the store, I noticed that the wall 'O coolers was all Pepsi products. Only one half of one door had Coke products. I grabbed the last two Diet Cokes they had. "That's an ugly trend." I said to James while waving in the general direction of the coolers. This was the first conscious recognition of "The Great Pepsi Conspiracy".

James had purchased a can of "Can Do" back in Dallas to clean the bikes before the rally. This stuff is an aerosol can and contains a high-quality wax and only Heaven knows what else. It claims to clean and shine everything…paint, chrome, tires, vinyl, windshields, helmets etc. I had tried it before we left and found that it worked pretty well, but thought no more about it.

Normally on a road trip if you want to make your bike look good sometime along the way, you have to carry some cleaning supplies. Chrome polish, wax, and Armor-all are usually in my arsenal. I also carry a can of Lemon-Pledge for my helmet. This is an old biker's trick. Lemon-Pledge cleans bugs and stuff of your faceplate like nothing else, and has the added benefit of making water bead up and blow off if you are in the rain. It also reduces the crazing you can usually see in the plastic face shield when riding into the sun. The problem is that space is limited, and all these products take up valuable and needed space.

Here comes a product endorsement: "Can Do" replaces all of those products, hands down. After washing the bikes in the car wash, mine was still a mess. The high-pressure spray, on soap, directed at my pipes from less than an inch away would not cut the baked on gook. Also the water there was extremely "hard" and left a bad film on both bikes.

Out came the "Can Do" and a couple of rags.

I sprayed this stuff on a section of my pipes and let it sit for about 30 seconds. The gook wiped right off, leaving shiny chrome underneath. No problem. Easy. I was stunned.

"Hey James, check this out." I did it again to another section. James was stunned. We had been talking about buying oven-cleaner for this task.

We then proceeded to wipe every part of both bikes down. In time we had two clean, shiny, and remarkable machines. You would never guess they had just traveled hundreds of miles, much less the mess mine had been earlier. This stuff works, and works well. It is all I will ever carry for this task in the future.

We headed for the rally grounds. James and I were both disappointed in the vendor selection at this rally. All I really wanted was a new pair of good warm-weather riding gloves. These are light leather, usually ventilated and used to protect your hands from mild abrasions, heat, sun, and windburn during summer riding. There were none there for sale.

No summer riding gloves. At a motorcycle rally. In the summer. Vendors are idiots.

Next I was looking for some leather shin/lower-leg guards. Remember the thump? I still do! One guy had some he would customize and sell for a small fortune. No normal ones to be found. The prices on everything else were unreasonable.

Oh…and the clincher…"The Great Pepsi Conspiracy" had reached the rally. "No Coke, Pepsi OK?" was the rallying cry. Only Pepsi and beer were to be found. Neither James nor I are heavy beer drinkers—especially when we are expecting to be riding motorcycles…duh…and Pepsi is *not* ok. If I wanted Pepsi, I would have asked for it by name.

Vendors, organizers, restaurant owners, convenience store operators take note—Pepsi better be paying you plenty, because all you are doing is antagonizing your customers by removing their choice and ability to purchase the #1 brand of drink in the state. Listen carefully…we left your location and made our purchases elsewhere over this issue. Plenty of other folks were also irritated. What the heck is the problem with carrying both?

Not sure what happened to the rest of Thursday, it sped by, and soon Friday was approaching. Friday was to be a busy day. James had signed us up for the group ride to Matamoros, Mexico. For 15 bucks each we would join a "limited" group of riders and cruise to Mexico. The cost covered border crossing fees, and a show and some food and drinks in Matamoros.

This was one of the highlights of the trip, and proved the Bike Fest folks to be very enterprising. Something like 1500 motorcycles were in the "limited" group. They staged us in lines of pairs of motorcycles in the Harlingen racetrack parking lot. When the signal was given to "start 'em up" the vibration must have set off earthquake detectors in California.

We then proceeded in a police escorted parade through Brownsville, across the border, and all around the streets of Matamoros. We got to run every stop-sign and stoplight on our route in two different countries. That alone was worth the 15 bucks. Folks were lined up all along the parade route waving flags and cheering. The people in Matamoros turned out by the tens of thousands. The streets were packed with cheering, screaming, flag-waving people. It really was amazing, and was a hell of an event for the folks that witnessed it. It got no news coverage in Brownsville.

We reached the Matamoros Convention center and staged again in the parking lot. Seven double-rows of 220 or so in each group. 1500-plus shiny and impressive pieces of hardware all lined up and ready to go.

They had several local restaurants providing food, and a couple of bands/singers providing entertainment. The cute young Mexican imitation of Britney Spears was good. The music was pop and upbeat, and delivered with passion. She was good looking too, and could wiggle in all the right places. Yummy. The food was excellent too, although my famous appetite suffered a bit as it had been a long, hot parade of over 40-miles. I tried Italian, Mexican, and Chinese. They had handed us two tickets each for drinks. "This looks bad." I said to James as I waved vaguely in the direction of the huge Pepsi sign, and thirty-foot blow up Pepsi balloon-can. Sure enough, no Coke.

We drank bottled water.

Now here is the part that proves the Bike Fest folks are enterprising...the other major event of the day in Matamoros was a bike show. 1500 bikes were now on display in the convention center parking lot! Throngs of people wandered through the shiny chrome maze. Matamoros police were on hand, but not needed. Everyone had a blast. Burly bikers were lifting families of kids (and their mothers too) onto and off of bikes and snapping pictures. A great time was had by all, and we favorably represented what it is to be an American to the friendly folks of Matamoros.

At one point I thought it was going to get ugly. I was sitting on my bike, talking to James and others that passed while we waited for the ride to head back. Six Matamoros Police Guys were in a group arguing amongst themselves while looking at my bike and gesturing in my direction. *Uh oh.* Finally one approached me. I was furiously trying to figure out what I had done to piss off the Mexican cops. I was honestly coming up empty handed. With some pointing, hand waving, and halting English he got across that the question concerned the year of my bike.

"1980." I said. Some more gesturing and a rapid exchange of Spanish with his cohorts ensued.

"1100?...XS?" he asked.

Surprised I answered, "Yep...Midnight Special."

"Gracias." he stated and waved as he rejoined his group. Laughter erupted and some money changed hands.

I was amazed to be noticed in this sea of $20,000 machines. Says something about the looks and reputation of the Midnight Special.

I must comment on the sea of bikes. I was flattered by the amount of attention "Well Oiled Machine" got. There were no other XS series bikes there. There were few older anythings there. Something like 1500 people were being independent minded bikers...in a very conformist sort of way. Brand-new Harleys ruled the day. There were hundreds and hundreds of the same model all over the place. "Well Oiled Machine" got attention because she was an attractive mote of "different" in a sea of sameness. Kind of sad really.

It was clearly illustrated when one couple mounted up nearby. "Shit!" exclaimed the guy to his girl. She was looking slightly perplexed. "Somebody stole your helmet!" he continued.

They sat there, mounted on the machine, for about 10 seconds. Finally she stated, "Honey, that's our bike over there." as she pointed to another "same" model with her helmet still sitting on the seat. Oops.

James and I glanced at each other with a raised eyebrow. No comment was needed. We were clearly thinking the same thing.

A couple of the other bikes that stood out should be mentioned:

There were two "Boss Hoss" bikes there. Check these out on the Internet if you have not seen them. A "Boss Hoss" is a motorcycle with a 350 cubic inch or larger Chevy engine stuffed in it. The sound of one of these things is impressive, and they will peel out like a demon on the full size car tire that is mounted on the back. Not sure what you would do with the other 250 extra horsepower. Interesting, nonetheless.

We also saw a small Triumph of unknown but old vintage. It was interesting as its rider was a very short (4'6") and very petite lady. She might have weighed 95 pounds sopping wet. This bike had to be kick started, and I would have bet she could not do it. I would have lost. She would stand on the lever in its full-up position and it would not move. She would then jump well above the seat and land her entire weight full on the lever. A couple of tries and the beast would pop to life. Maybe one woman in ten thousand would try something like that. Interesting. I like interesting people.

The signal was given, the earthquake roared to life. We pulled out and paraded back through the streets of Matamoros. Again, tens of thousands of people turned out. What an ego trip.

The American crossing is a mess. This is partly because of the recent events, but mostly because we are a bureaucratic nightmare of a nation and getting worse. We are just not very good at this sort of stuff, and it is made worse because we just do not care. The Americans have the traffic backed up for miles waiting to get into the States. Thousands of bikers clearly would have made the situation intolerable, so we got to go across the border on a railroad bridge. 1500 motorcycles fleeing Mexico across the railroad tracks. What a blast.

To sum it up: We went to Mexico. We drank the water. We escaped over a railroad bridge. A great time was had by all.

Once across border the parade broke apart in a spectacularly rapid fashion and was absorbed into Brownsville. One humorous note was when one of the parade section leaders with about 15 riders in tow, pulled up beside us at a stoplight. "Which way to the highway?"

Hell, we didn't know. We were just cruising vaguely in the direction we needed to go, and checking out Brownsville. Holistic navigation. Since we were at the absolute most southern tip of Texas, we figured if you go north you would be pretty much covered.

"I think it's up there...hang a left at the overpass." I yelled back.

"No. I think you turn right up ahead." the section leader called back. That would be south, and back into Mexico. They roared off. I shrugged and grinned at James. I have visions of this lost group of bikers, forever faithfully following a section leader who has no idea where they are going. Hope they find someplace interesting.

The only regret we have for attending the Matamoros ride is that we missed the amateur bike show. I wanted to see what sort of bikes show up there, as they have a "classic cruiser" category for 20–25 year old bikes that "Well Oiled Machine" could probably place in...but I want to check out the competition at one of these before I enter. "Well Oiled Machine" is a head turner, but I may really be outclassed. Still do not know.

Friday night Blue Oyster Cult and REO Speedwagon were playing. This was the optional (extra $$) concert and we did not purchase tickets for it. It was just a bit pricey. REO is one of my favorite groups, but we were also kind-of worried about the "geriatric rock band reunion" phenomenon. Would have killed my memories if they rolled them out on stage in wheelchairs or something. Turned out we did not need to worry. We could clearly hear REO from the fairgrounds. They had not lost it.

Dinner at Denny's...Pot-roast and ice-cream sundaes for dessert. For some reason the pot roast at Denny's is amazing. Saturday was the poker-run, so we had to be up early. After a soak in the hotel's hot tub I slept the sleep of the dead again. What a trip.

For those that do not know what a poker run is, you are given instructions from a starting point to five destinations to be ridden to in order. At each destination they stamp your sheet or give you a token, and you move on to the next stop. When complete at the final destination they check your stamps, then you get to draw a poker hand. There are usually prizes for the best hand, second place, and sometimes the worst hand, but prizes are not really the point. The run is arranged so that the ride is scenic, and the stops are interesting.

The first stop on this run was an air museum and a waffle breakfast. They had WWII era planes flying overhead and doing stunts. Fun. Museums usually depress me though. They had a PBY (massive amphibious plane, it was a workhorse during WW II and is really an amazing airplane) parked out back. It was a lonely, rotting hulk, and it was obvious that it would never fly again. Sad. That's no way for a machine to go.

After leaving there we needed a drink. We stopped at a convenience store along the route. There were no Coke products at all in the store. Not even any place for them. The operator seemed exasperated when I asked where they were.

We went elsewhere. The next store had one small cooler of Coke products. They also had Diet Coke with lemon. I had not seen this product before and tried it. I like it.

One stop was a barbeque place/biker bar. They were out of barbeque. James had a burger, I had the spicy wings. Not too bad. Cute waitress.

This poker run was about 100 miles and with the stops and our typical dawdling around and sightseeing took several hours.

Back at the fairgrounds we drew our hands. We did not win, my hand probably should have won worst hand and James drew three-of-a-kind...threes I think. But no matter, riding is the point, yes?

We visited the professional bike show. Ten bikes or so. Amazing paint jobs, and obviously a lot of work had gone into them. These bikes were built from the ground up, but the result was basically all the same bike! Again, expressing our independence and artistry…in a conformist sort of way. Boring. I left without being able to choose a "people's choice" favorite. None stood out. I find this disturbing.

There was also a parade Saturday afternoon. Much like the Matamoros ride, except it went from the Iwo-Jima monument to the fairgrounds in Harlingen. It was also about three times the size of the Matamoros run. At least 4500 bikes participated and it stretched for miles. The rumble was incredible. Not a car alarm in range could stay silent. The news stated that "500 bikers showed up". Interesting. Get it right guys.

Included in the registration package were tickets to the 38-Special concert Saturday night. I am slightly embarrassed that we did not attend. We ate dinner, went back to the hotel, and soaked in the hot tub for a couple hours.

Zonk.

PART FOUR—THE JOURNEY HOME

We slept late Sunday, then packed up and pulled out. Looking at the map, we decided that we could go back through Laredo and avoid that horrendously boring stretch of road on US 281. We headed west out of Harlingen on US 83. This route would add something like 70 miles to our trip, but it was a small price to pay.

At Laredo we turned north on Interstate 35 for a short stretch, planning to leave it onto US 83 in about 20 miles.

In that stretch we hit a Border Patrol checkpoint. They have all traffic on Interstate 35 pull off into lines, and they check you out. While we waited in line I pulled beside James. I constantly tease him about all the trunks on his 'Wing. "You got any illegal aliens stuffed in there?"

He reached back and thumped the right side bag. "Shut up in there, you're going to get caught."

The checkpoint reminded me of something out of a WWII movie. Men with guns and dogs stopping all traffic. I am fairly ruthless about my rights. Where I am going and what I am doing is not the business of anybody in authority, unless and until I have been proven to have done something wrong. James and I are apparently the minority these days…as we are unwilling to sacrifice our rights and freedoms in the name of security.

These guys had dogs, and were checking out some vehicles. Apparently those dogs hate motorcycles. I mean *really* hate motorcycles. As we approached the checkpoint, one of the dogs went nuts. It was struggling to reach us and barking and howling furiously. Spittle was flying from its lips. Its handler wrapped the lead twice around the porch railing of their small office. The handler would not have been able to hold it back otherwise. The dog was leaping and shaking the entire porch each time it was jerked up short by its lead. The handler seemed somewhat bored, so I assume this is a common occurrence. Glad he was able to control it.

When we reached the guy at the gate, he asked James, "You a US Citizen?"

"No." says James as he is nodding his head yes.

"Thanks. Have a good day." says the guy as he waves him on.

I pull up. "You a US Citizen?" asks the guy.

"Huh?" says I.

"Thanks. Have a good day." he says as he waves me on.

That is terribly effective. They should save everybody the trouble and just put a sign on the highway saying "Terrorists, Smugglers, Drug Dealers Exit Here." That would be just as effective and the rest of us could go about our business.

Oh well.

We hit US 83 and headed north. A few miles in James passed a slow moving 18-wheeler. I got stuck behind it for a while due to traffic and hills and visibility. When the opportunity came I tweaked the throttle and shot around. James was very far ahead so I did not let off the throttle immediately. As I neared him I began to slow and pull into position. I glanced down at the speedometer. Holy cow! 130 mph. *Sheesh.*

A few minutes later a juxtaposition of events made for some fun. I was starting to doubt that my speedometer had really said 130 mph. We crested a small hill and looked forward to at least 15 miles of road, slightly uphill, with both sides of the road clearly visible the entire way. There was no traffic in sight and had been none since we passed the truck some miles back. At that moment a particularly rollicking tune started on my mp3 player.

"Well Oiled Machine" chose that moment to get frisky.

"Come on. Let's go." she clearly said.

"Can't, I'm following James." I responded.

"Got to go. Got to go now. Got to. Got to. Got to. Go faster. *Must* go faster." she insisted. I'll have to watch that super unleaded gas...I think it has caffeine in it.

"Ok." I am a pushover for a beautiful woman.

I tweaked the throttle and shot past James. He would have no problem knowing what I was up to. The road in front of us was self-explanatory.

I never hit full throttle. Within seconds she was at 135 mph and the tachometer was redlined at 8500 rpm. She was still accelerating and showed no sighs of running out of power, but I let off, as I did not want to go over the redline.

"Well Oiled Machine" was smooth and stable, with no unusual vibration or shimmy. I held the speed for a few moments, but was soon cresting the hill. I let off it and gradually slowed back down to 75 mph or so. She is an incredible machine. The torque and power available are nothing short of amazing.

James zoomed by a moment later and again took the lead. We later found another open space and he pushed it up to 100 mph and held it there a while. He had to ask later how fast he took us to…his speedometer only goes to 85 mph. Mine goes to 160 mph! Gives you an attitude.

After the rain we encountered out of Dallas, the rest of our trip had been absolutely perfect weather. You could not have asked for nicer days, and today was no exception.

The miles flew by, but so did the time. A couple of fuel stops later darkness was upon us and we were still 100 miles out of Kerrville. Oh well. Don the jackets and take off.

The short way was the fun way this time. Some small backroad between US 83 and Kerrville promised twisties. Kewl. Twisties. In the dark. In deer country. Should be interesting.

This road was extremely twisty, with one-lane bridges and lots of up and down…sometimes way, way down into low water crossings. We dodged lots of wildlife. One was a skunk.

As James describes it, "Oh shit! A skunk!" as he is taking evasive action. Then, "Oh crap…it's facing the wrong direction!"

Fortunately neither of us got sprayed.

Halfway through this 100-mile stretch, we pulled off the side of the road for a break. Twisties in the dark takes lots of tension and concentration. We had to get off the bikes. I was starting to cramp up.

We could hear water running in the valley below the road, but nothing else. There were no cars out here. Spooky. Neat. James smoked a cigar, and when we were rested we mounted up and took off.

James stopped after 100 feet or so. He had taken his glasses off to put on his helmet, and set them on his tank. He had forgotten to put them back on. He rapidly figured that out, as he cannot see to drive without them. Bad news.

I turned my bike around and went back to what I was sure was well before the spot we had been pulled off at. I turned the bike around and parked it back in the grass on the side of the road. I left the headlight on. The glasses were not on the road. That meant that they were in the grass. I grabbed the flashlight and slowly walked all the way to where James was stopped in the road ahead. No sign of them.

I turned around and along with James, slowly walked all the way back to my bike, carefully scanning for the glasses.

"They can't be under anything." commented James.

"Unless they're under my bike." I joked.

Slowly we looked at each other. Distances are deceiving in the dark.

"Oh shit." we both said in unison.

Slowly I swung the flashlight around.

The glasses were there, full up against my back tire. They were not the slightest damaged or scratched. Amazing luck. I missed running over them not just once, but twice!

Soon we pulled into Kerrville. Pot roast and ice cream sundaes at Denny's again. While fishing the last of the hot fudge out of my sundae, I glanced at James. He looked thoughtful. I had a good idea what about as I had been thinking about the last stretch of road. Twisties are a blast. "Want to go again?" I asked with a grin.

"Yeah. Yeah I do."

Home Stretch:

Si woke us up with breakfast again. Once again, the mountain of scrambled eggs, frying pan full of home-made sausage, and huge stack of toast stood no chance of surviving our assault.

We pulled out of Kerrville on Texas 16 and this time cut over to US 281 on 1383…a small and twistie of 30 miles or so. This was fun, but was interesting as it was open range land. We crossed a cattle guard, and after that there were no fences at all. Some bloody big beef was wandering around in there.

The grasshoppers made for an interesting trip through here. It was quite cool, and grasshoppers by the thousands were all over the road, sunning themselves. They did not bother James in the slightest, as he was leading. His passage would disturb them and they would leap into the air…just in time to smack into me. Splat. I backed off, but that did not help, as they were inevitably on their second leap. I backed way off, but then they were on their third leap. Splat, smack, crunch, splatter, splut by the dozens. Ghack! This was intolerable! Eventually I found the exact distance behind James, where they had already leaped and landed, but not had time for the second leap.

We hit US 281, gassed up in Johnson City, and headed north. We had just left the town, and had climbed to highway speed. The road here was not divided and was two lanes in each direction. We were traveling in our usual formation in the left-hand lane.

Directly in front of James an oncoming 18-wheeler suddenly swerved completely into our lane. James and I instantly and simultaneously executed a very hard right, in perfect formation. We then had to flop over and go hard left to avoid driving off the side of the road. One mistake from either of us and a pile of bikes would have tumbled off the road (at best) or under the oncoming 60,000-pound truck (uh…that would be worst). The coordinated evasive turns must have been a beautiful sight, had there been anybody else around to see them. These were high speed, peg-dragging turns, and we barely cleared the truck. A car would have been annihilated. After we were back in our groove, I glanced in my mirrors. The truck had gone clear across both of our lanes, and was headed back to the other side of the road. His brake lights were on. Maybe he blew a tire. Whew.

The miles evaporated and soon we were back on US 67. At Keene hunger hit and we searched for something to eat. A Sonic at the end of town proved to be brand-new and still under construction. It was not open yet, and the rest of town looked pretty bleak. Sitting at a stoplight I could see three different donut stores…there had to be someplace to eat dinner somewhere. The stoplight changed and James roared off and made a left turn into a shopping center. He had spotted a small place with the imaginative title of "Restaurant" barely painted on the front. It would have to do.

We both ordered chicken-fried steaks, and Diet Coke! They actually had it. Thank heavens the "Great Pepsi Conspiracy" had not reached the Dallas area in our absence.

The last note of humor on this ride was the old local guy in the restaurant that asked me excitedly "What are you riding?"

Fresh from days on the road, brimming with the experience, I have never been prouder of my machine. I replied readily, "A 1980 Midnight Special."

His face fell. You could tell he was intensely disappointed. "I had you pegged for a Harley guy." He mumbled.

I puzzled over this for a moment or two. I was still puzzling over this when we rode out of town. Until I looked down and realized I was wearing my riding jeans. Although they had been laundered, they were still obviously oil-stained up to the knee on the left leg, and over the ankle on the right. Although Harley owners are loathe to admit it, Harleys used to be notorious for leaking oil. It is usually a point of pride that the Japanese bikes do not.

I have not laughed so hard in months.

1934 miles. *One-thousand-nine-hundred and thirty-four miles.*

As I took leave of James at his place I asked him with a grin, "Want to go again?"

One-thousand-nine-hundred and thirty-four miles. Any normal person would be ready to park the bike and not look at it for a while. Any normal person. He looked back out toward the road and gave the expected answer. The only answer.

"Yeah…Yeah I do."

Wheelie (Oh my Gawd!)

There are times when riding a motorcycle, that you are pushed to the limits of your ability…and occasionally beyond them.

I have a 1980 Midnight Special, nicknamed "Well Oiled Machine". This is an 1100cc shaft-drive bike and is quite powerful, both for her size and for the era in which she was built. A common misperception among less experienced motorcyclists is that shaft driven bikes will not do a wheelie, that is, will not pull the front wheel off the ground with its raw power and acceleration. Now I am an experienced motorcyclist, and I know that if you should want to, you can easily get a shaft drive bike to wheelie. Personally I am usually a much more conservative rider than that and find little desire or occasion to run a wheelie on a street bike.

Some are still skeptical. Well Oiled Machine is over 20 years old and heavily traveled. I am 6' and 300 pounds, but yes, she will do a wheelie even with me on her.

It went something like this:

Driving down the street…one of those surface streets, three lanes each direction. Almost get run over by some guy in a Jeep Cherokee as he changed rapidly/violently into my lane (I was in the right hand lane). Extreme braking, thanks to my newly revamped brakes and stainless-steel brake lines, lets me barely eeek in behind him. Guess he was not looking eh? Another car beside, and coming to a stop light, so I get stuck behind him for the light.

The light turns green, all other cars take off. The Cherokee just sits. I pull into the now empty middle lane to go around and from a standing stop he guns it and changes into my lane again. All but got me. I do not think I have ever come closer.

Now, I don't know that this asshole was trying to kill me or anything, but almost run over by the same guy twice inside of 30 seconds is not a good thing.

I figure I have had enough of this guy, need to let him go away. I stop in the street. There are no cars coming from behind.

Well, now the Cherokee stops. *Uh Oh…*

Then his reverse lights come on. *Um…Urrk…*

As he starts to back up I gun it and change back into the right lane. Cleared him by at least 4 inches. That XS will lay a hell of a scratch, and boy will she move! I get around him, and take off down the road. This was a 45 mph zone. I figure 80 mph will ditch the jeep.

Now I am approaching another light. There is only one car in the left lane. Slowing down for the red light, I glance in the mirrors. Here comes the jeep, and fast.

Now I a patient man, but I have had enough. I left my grenade launcher at home so I figure I am going to "BUG" out. "BUG" is a motorcyclist's unit of measurement that is defined as the speed at which bugs will begin to stick/splat to you instead of bouncing off. I believe it is generally accepted to be 50 mph.

I figure "BUG3" ought to do it.

Look ahead to see what my options are, and the light changes to green. I have free lanes and I *know* the XS will do 135 mph (see *SPI Bike Fest*).

I think I was still doing about 30 mph or so. Dumped it down a couple of gears to second and gave it full throttle. I have never been able to use full throttle before.

The sound barrier and the light-speed barrier were immediately shattered…at least it seemed that way to me anyway.

The front wheel started to come up…I have never done that before, but it felt stable so I covered the back brake and said, "What the hell."

I rode it for a few seconds, and shifted up once. She was still pulling and still up. When I shifted again the front started to drop. I remember glancing at the speedometer and thinking, *sure feels like I am going a lot faster than 50.* Took a microsecond or so to remember that the speedometer reads the front wheel, and the front wheel was off the ground. Adrenaline. *Sheesh.*

Shifted into fifth and the wheel dropped back to the ground. For the first time I ran her over the red-line. When I let off the speed was 140mph.

Wow. "Bug2.8". Not bad.

I never saw the jeep again.

Man can that bike move. She *rocks.* I think it took longer to get slowed down than it did to get going that fast.

My thoughts immediately afterward:

That was really, really cool…and I am never doing that, ever again, and, *Where the hell is a rocket launcher when you really need one?*

Passing the Torch

The "Well Oiled Rider" of "Well Oiled Machine" here...

Some sadness, but good news nonetheless:

Those of you that know me remember the exploits encountered in slowly resurrecting my daily driven 1980 XS-1100SG Midnight Special, "Well Oiled Machine", from her previous owner's incompetence and severe neglect.

Those exploits include many thousands of miles, a "Revolutionary In-flight Oil Change Method" (*not* highly recommended), a taste test of hot Castroil 15w-40, and a massive oil spill covering most of South Texas (2 incidents, and I have plausible deniability if the EPA comes calling).

After two years of hard riding and lots of wrenching "Well Oiled Machine" was back to her original glory. New polyurethane black paint and new chrome were the finishing touches. A 160 mph speedometer, sport fairing, stainless brake lines, fork brace, and her rider all gave her an attitude. She really sticks out in a crowd. It is not really necessary to actually drive on the front wheel if you do not want to (wheelies...woohoo!)

"Bug 2.8" was achieved...once...and "Bug 2.7" is easily possible and does not even cause a strain.

For those that do not know, "Bug" is a motorcyclist's unit of measurement. It is defined as the speed where bugs start to stick/splat to you instead of bouncing off. "Bug" is generally accepted to be 50 miles-per-hour.

Folks may also remember that I bought "The Dragon" in December or so of last year. "The Dragon" is a 2001 Honda 1520 F6 Valkyrie.

This is the first new bike I have ever owned. I've paid my dues, and cannot believe that I waited so long.

Well, bikes all have personalities and soul, and the one thing they require above all else is that they be ridden, hard and frequently. They are in Purgatory if they are not. That's no way for a machine to exist.

On the rare occasions when I was not actually riding, "Well Oiled Machine" and "The Dragon" sat in the garage and growled at each other. When it came time to ride (and that is very often for me) both machines vied for my attention with sometimes blatant plays on my emotions. Whatever the choice, I somehow felt that I had let the other machine down.

Leaving a machine weeping in the dark garage on a sunny day or a balmy night can be heart wrenching.

I happened to mention my dilemma to a friend that I work with who had been aware of my history with this bike, and he was interested in taking "Well Oiled Machine" for a spin. I was surprised, as I was unaware he was a rider, and usually I can spot a rider immediately—in whatever guise. But it turns out he is and it was obviously a good match.

Today he cut me a check. "Well Oiled Machine" is his. The weather has been gorgeous, in the 70's at night and 80's during the day. Letting him ride *that* bike, with its power, agility, looks, and attitude—in *this* weather—it was probably a foregone conclusion. The time has come to pass the torch.

"Well Oiled Machine" is going to a good home, and will be ridden frequently. Myself, my friend, "Well Oiled Machine", and "The Dragon" are all much happier now. Everybody wins.

I have always purchased older, well-used bikes and fixed them up. Then I would drive them until there was just nothing left to fix. This is the first bike I have sold that was still in operable condition.

I spent a lot of hours and elbow grease restoring "Well Oiled Machine" to her former glory. She is in every way a good solid bike.

My friend is getting a good machine and I have the freedom to ride "The Dragon."

So why do I feel guilty?

Valkyrie Magic

There are some things in this world that are not so easily explained.

Title if News Headline: "Valkyries Reportedly Attract Naked Women—Honda Sales Up 3875%."

I was headed north…just north, and I was moving fast. I am not being vague, "north" was the extent of my planning for this journey. In fact, I had not planned this journey at all. I had left work in downtown Dallas, donned my riding gear, mounted my Valkyrie and hit the highway. I had actually been headed home, but could not bring myself to make the exit. Not now. Not today. I was tired, very tired. I was mentally burned out, and too much had happened.

There is a certain magic to the Valkyrie. Any that own one probably already know. Nicknamed "The Dragon" she carries me effortlessly to anywhere I wish to go. I have ridden many machines, but none like this one. None have ever fit me so well in size, personality, and temperament. I *ride* other machines, I *become* "The Dragon". Smooth, fast, and powerful, with a mystique all her own, she both carries me and becomes a part of me. An expansion of my awareness. An extension of my blood, bone, and muscle. With the smooth power and aggressive rumble of this superb machine below me, after a few miles of riding, the machine, and through her the road, become a part of myself.

There are times when you just have to ride. Anyone that does or has ridden a motorcycle knows this. It is both an addiction, and it is a cure.

It is an addiction in that when you are not riding you are thinking about riding. When you are not on a road-trip you are planning the next one. I have returned from a two thousand-mile excursion, only to look back out at the road and sigh. I want to go again. Now. Not at some later date. *Now.* Those of us in the extreme stages of the addiction become mildly upset or feel that we have somehow failed when we actually take the "cage" (car or truck) somewhere instead of the bike.

For all it demands as an addiction, riding pays you back many times over by being a cure. Riding will lighten your mood, and curb your anxieties. It will calm you, crystallize your thinking, and organize your mind. If everyone rode, there would be no need for psychiatrists…and probably much less need for lawyers.

Today was one of those days when I needed all of the benefits of riding. And I needed them badly. Work is always chaotic…I work in the Information Technology portion of a major newspaper…effectively combining two of the most stressful jobs known to man. We start with nothing everyday, and then apply impossible deadlines and throw in a critical crisis or two just for good measure. In my case, work demands far more of my effort, concentration, creativity and…well…my soul than I can continually give. Without some sort of balance, it can eventually destroy me. Every once and a while life and work fall out of balance, it just catches up with me.

Today was one of those days. I love my job and the people I work with, but fourteen hours of this place will drive anyone to want to get away. Multiple crises and impossible deadlines, again. I had had enough. There was nothing left within me to give. I dropped what I was doing, logged out, and left the building. No need to explain to the boss, I got here long before he did, and he was already gone.

When I stepped outside I found the weather absolutely perfect for riding. It was about 75 degrees, breezy, and a bit humid. The sky was clear and there was nearly a full moon. This sort of weather is fairly normal for a night in Texas, but not so common in January. Shirt-sleeve riding weather in January, I *do* love those Texas winters.

Nights like this stir certain feelings within me, and practically demand that I ride. The feelings are deep and primal, originating far within and infusing my entire being. They are not controllable or suppressible, and are quite unlike anything else I ever experience, and that makes them very hard to effectively describe. I think "horniness" would not be too far off the mark, although that is not quite it. Definitely related though.

Traffic had been light, and the freeway had really been moving. I was headed north out of Dallas on US 75, passed my exit, and simply just kept going. Twenty-some miles later, just north of McKinney, I could make out a long line of brake-lights and some flashing police lights ahead. Something had happened and shut the highway down. Nope. I needed to ride—this would not do at all. I pulled a hard right and caught the exit I had nearly passed, scattering gravel from the shoulder and spinning off onto US 121/Texas 5. Shortly afterward the two highways separated and I took the highway 5 branch, simply because it looked darker in that direction.

I passed through Melissa, which is a one-horse town with delusions of becoming a two-horse one someday soon. Their abortive attempt at having a police force and town services funded by highly questionable speed traps brings the campy 70's show, *The Dukes of Hazzard* to mind, and is legend in these parts, but that is subject for another story.

I know this area somewhat and am aware that after some miles of empty road come the towns of Anna, Van Alstyne, Howe, and then the city of Sherman. Sherman is still about 40 miles ahead of me. Somewhere in there I will need to stop for gas. An inkling of a plan begins to form. Maybe I'll grab a bite to eat in Sherman and then, if my mood will allow me to, I'll head home. It is still not a certain plan, as I am still not sure why I am even out here to begin with, other than to ride.

I am finally beginning to relax. I am somewhere between Anna and Van Alstyne, and find myself amazed at how tense I am. The best way I can describe it is that I felt sick in my soul. Stretched thin. I was having difficulty imagining how I could return to work. Not only how I could, but why I would. I have many dreams for the future, and my job is necessary at this time to further them, but I am just not ready right now. It does not seem worth it.

I am pulling 80 mph or so, and am reveling in the beautiful night air, and in the sensations of the powerful machine that has now become an extension of my being. It helps, but somehow, tonight, it is just not enough.

Motorcyclists are generally very alert to what is going on around them. They are sensitive to the road, the traffic, and the machine they have become a part of. They are also really hooked into life in general and the world around them. Just *being* has become an intimate experience.

Adult males are also naturally and inevitably sensitive to certain things. There are objects in this world that immediately and without fail, attract and hold the attention of a male.

Powerful, mystical, and undeniable, these two forces normally do not combine. Tonight was to be different, and given the circumstances outlined above, make some of the following events inevitable.

I was on a lonely stretch of road. There were no lights other than the moon and stars, and I had not encountered any traffic in at least 10 minutes. Far ahead of me a figure stepped out of the brush and stood on the shoulder of the road. The figure was still far out of my headlight range, but was visible as a stunning and marvelous silhouette in the bright moonlight.

Several things were revealed to the hypersensitive motorcyclist and/ or the male within me. The figure was a she, she was shapely, and she was nude. I immediately took my hand off the gas and began to decelerate.

The following is a "conversation" between several sides of my brain. All this happened in a micro-second, and is probably completely pointless, as apparently the decision to stop had already been made. I was already slowing down, and she was just beginning to come into view in my headlight.

The Analytical Brain: *Whoa guys, get off the brake get your hand back on the gas. Something is wrong here.*

The Motorcyclist: *Somebody is standing beside the road. She may be in trouble.*

The Texan: *She needs help. Let's stop.*

The Male: *There is a naked women beside the road. We're stopping.*

The Analytical Brain: *All I'm saying is that something is up. We should go on. People just do not step out into the road. This could be a trap.*

The Motorcyclist: *There is no sign of an accident, and we have not passed any broken down cars. There are no houses anywhere near here. Maybe he's right, something is up.*

The Texan: *She needs help. Let's stop.*

The Male: *Did you guys not hear me? There is a naked women beside the road!*

The Analytical Brain: *We're not stopping. This is some sort of ambush. Wait…did you say naked?*

The Motorcyclist: *No sign of anybody else around. We really should go on. Um…naked? She really is naked?*

The Texan: *She needs help. Let's stop.*

The Male: *Naked. As in nude. And she's a redhead! Oh wow, a natural redhead!*

The Analytical Brain: *Stop.*

The Motorcyclist: *Stop.*

The Texan: *Stop.*

The Male: *Yeah, no shit.*

I pulled to a stop beside the woman on the road. There is not a red-blooded male…no real man on the planet…that could have done otherwise.

She is standing there, a hand half raised to wave me down. She is healthy, shapely, and toned. Curvy in all the right places. Just over 5 feet tall or so. She has long dark-red hair done in a large braid, and hanging down to the small of her back. As the male in me noted as soon as she was visible in my headlight, she is actually a real natural redhead. She has green eyes, and they are very vivid considering they get my attention in the light of the moon…and despite other, more obvious distractions. By the standard societal illusion of beauty, her breasts are just on the small side. The have a little sag to them, indicating that she is not just barely 18 or pumped full of silicone. Her nipples are erect in the night air. Her face is a little square. Her eyes are framed by a few stray red hairs. All combine to make her a startlingly beautiful woman.

She is standing there almost proudly, maybe defiantly. She is not ashamed of her nakedness—it would have been pointless to try to hide it—but still she manages to look slightly flighty…a little unsure of her situation. Not really fear, but maybe caution, tempered with confidence. Her bearing, along with her obvious attributes combine to render an impression that is remarkably sensual. I would place her to be about 30, and her bearing and obvious health shows she is not a prostitute or addict.

I do not know her story, but instinctively know it is not a typical one.

I hit the kill switch on the bike and remove my helmet. A detached part of me notes that her feet are bleeding a little, and I can see the footprints where she stepped onto the road. Cross-country in Texas scrub-land, or on asphalt and gravelly highway shoulders is no place to walk in bare feet. Another detached part of me is amazed that I am noticing anything at all other than the rather obvious. She really projects…well…life and sensuality.

We size each other up.

Her beautiful green eyes look intently and unblinkingly into my blue ones.

"Well?" she asks liltingly but defiantly. She has a mild and interesting accent…hard to identify. Maybe Irish.

"Nice night for a walk." I say easily. The situation is obviously odd, and we both know it. Given a perfect world, neither of us would be here, in this situation, at this location, right now. It is unnecessary to point it out.

She seems somewhat relieved. Apparently I have passed some kind of test. She waits, content to let me make the next move. Being a typical guy, I could wait too, being perfectly content to languish there just taking in the...well...scenery, but I feel the need to move on. I am still not really ok inside.

Carefully I ask her, "How can I help you?" Again it is obvious that she needs some help. No real need to ask anything else. She will tell what she feels she needs to.

"I do not wish to disrupt your plans, but I need a ride to the lake if you please."

"The lake" was obvious. She was talking about Lake Texhoma, one of the largest man-made lakes in the country. Lake Texhoma is about 20 miles north of Sherman, and is huge. It is long and skinny, running several hundred miles in length from east to west along the border between Texas and Oklahoma. The dam, which is on the east end, is just north of Sherman. A ride to "the lake" from here could be as short as 30 minutes, or as long as 5 hours, depending on where she needed to go.

I vaguely indicate the cell phone on my belt. "Sure you do not need me to call the police?" and as I motion toward her feet, "Or perhaps an ambulance?"

She laughs lightly. She has a nice voice, and beautiful laugh. I am pleased to see her smile. That indicates that whatever has happened, it probably was not horribly serious.

"No. I have not been harmed. And these are just scratches. The last thing I need is for the police to show up. A very few may understand, fewer still would help. Most are just school-yard ruffians."

My respect for her climbs another notch or two. Her opinion of the police mirrors my own, and many women in her situation, whatever that may be, would be hysterical.

She looks at me mischievously, "I have no money with which to pay you…"

Well…that at least was obvious. It is my turn to laugh. "I guessed as much, and money you do not need. You are in Texas, and I am a Texan." I wave toward my bike and myself with a flourish, "For beautiful naked women, rides on the Dragon are always free. No strings attached."

She smiles at me, and her eyes shine in the moonlight, "Somehow I knew."

I grin back. "I'm Daniel by the way. Nice to meet you."

"Hello Dan-ie-yel." Her accent rendered my name musically and with three syllables. "I am Cat."

Cat…It figures…It fit.

I kick the stand down and climb off the bike. I remove my leather jacket. It has really been too warm for it anyhow, and I have been riding with it mostly open. As I help her into it I cannot help but again admire her figure and her bearing. The male in me is wide awake and obviously so, but the Texan is in charge. This is going to be a long night.

I am a big guy, and my leather jacket swallows her nearly down to her knees. The night scenery suddenly gets a whole lot less attractive. Sigh. I had almost left the jacket home that morning.

She indicates the Valkyrie. The big cruiser shines and makes a unique statement, even in the moonlight. "The Dragon is she? She is gorgeous." She eyes me critically for a moment. Nods. "She suits you."

My respect for her climbs even higher. "Have you ridden before?"

"Yes." She looks wistfully at the bike, then back at the road. I know the look. She is seeing different times, other adventures. She brings herself back to the present. Smiles again. "It has been a while though."

She belts the jacket closed. It is too big on her to just zip it up.

I mount up. "Climb aboard then." I pop the passenger pegs down, and warily eye her bare feet and legs. "Watch the pipes."

She smiles again. "I'll be careful."

I give her the helmet and she climbs aboard. "I'll have to stop for gas soon." I tell her as I start the engine.

As I pull back onto the road and accelerate she hugs me around the waist and says, "Perfect. I'm famished anyway."

I push it up to about 80 mph and rocket into the night, again reveling in the power of my mount. Slowly I become aware of a sensation being transmitted to me from her. First I thought she was trembling. She could be cold, although the night air was really quite comfortable. I finally realize that she is singing. I wish I could hear.

Between gusts of wind I hear a snatch or two of her song. She has a nice singing voice. I almost slow the bike, so I can hear more clearly, but somehow feel that would be intruding.

Nothing obvious presents itself for a decent place to stop in the next few miles. About 20 miles from Sherman the Valkyrie begins to lose power, and the engine changes tone. I reach down just inside my left thigh and switch the big bike to reserve. The power immediately comes back and we continue to roar into the night. The Valkyrie has about 1.5 gallons of reserve fuel. We still can go a long way before fuel is a problem.

We finally approach the lights of the city. Sherman is a mid-sized town, so has plenty of places open after typical hours. I pull into one for some gas. She lithely climbs off the bike saying, "I'll just be a jiff." Getting off the passenger's position on a Valkyrie without so much as brushing the hot pipes with your bare legs and feet involves several acrobatic and quite revealing moves when you are wearing a very large and loosely belted leather jacket with absolutely nothing underneath.

With a start, and a loud clatter, the guy in the orange Ford pickup at the next pump drops the gas hose and his gas cap. As he reaches down to pick it up, all the while looking at Cat…while trying not to look like he is looking at Cat, he bangs his head on the concrete filled pole that protects the pump from errant cars.

Cat smiles at him and winks at me as she heads off to the ladies' room. As she passes the guy in the orange Ford, her loosely belted jacket flaps open briefly.

Muffled cursing comes from the guy from the orange Ford as he again drops the gas hose and bangs his head on the same pole, but I ignore it. I can identify, watching her out of sight and thinking that the name "Cat" really does suit her.

I sigh, and after a moment fumble around in my wallet for my credit card. Before I can slide it into the pump, the guy from the orange Ford slides his own card through the slot. He is smiling.

"Allow me to buy, you and The Lady have just made my night. Perhaps my month."

I eye the already obvious bump growing on his forehead. I would bet he is going to have a heck of a black eye. "You sure you're all right?"

He smiles again and rubs his head as Cat approaches. "Never better. Take care of Her. Have a nice night."

As he walks away he says back over his shoulder, "Nice bike by the way."

Hmmm. Nice guy. Must be a Texan.

I top off the bike, switch her back off reserve, and look at Cat. She is looking back at me. Finger toying with her bottom lip.

"You hungry?" I ask her.

She takes a deep breath. The resulting motions are mind-boggling. "Absolutely famished."

"Where would you like to eat?"

She looks slightly confused, "I know not. Anything. Anywhere."

There is a Denny's just up the street. I know they will be open. For those of you not familiar with Denny's, they are a nationwide chain of short-order restaurants. Their main claim to fame is that they are always open. The food is pretty good and the service is usually okay. For some reason the pot roast is spectacular.

We move to the Denny's. There are not many customers, and the hostess warily eyes Cat, but seats us nonetheless.

The waitress comes to take our order. "Something to drink?"

Then she notices Cat's bare feet and revealing dress. With false sweetness the waitress looks at me and says, "I'm sorry sir, store policy says no bare feet allowed."

I look at Cat wondering what she wants to eat. She is looking at me and smiling. She seems to know what I am thinking. "I trust you." She mouths silently.

I look back at the waitress. I have played this role before. I am six feet, and nearly 300 pounds. A fair amount of that is muscle. I will not be moved involuntarily and the person that can intimidate me has yet to be born. "That's nice dear. We'll both have iced tea. Thanks."

Flustered, she retreats. I can see her talking to some guy in the back. Probably the manager. I see him look our way, then do a double take when he gets a good look at Cat. Our iced teas arrive via the manager in record time.

"What'll you folks have?" He asks pleasantly, all the while trying not to look at Cat. He could have saved himself the trouble. Cat is worth looking at, and it doesn't seem to phase her.

"Two orders of pot-roast. Mashed potatoes, carrots, and we'll have hot fudge sundaes for dessert."

"Good choice. We'll have it up shortly sir."

We proceeded to have the best meal and best service I have ever encountered at a Denny's. We talk of many things. Life, the world, and the differences and dependencies between men and women. As I attempted to pay the check the manager took it from me. "It's on me sir. Take care of the lady. You folks have a nice night."

On the way out I grinned at Cat. "I am going to have to take beautiful nude women out to dinner more often."

Her delightful laugh is my reward.

Following Cat's somewhat vague directions we wound our way out of Texas to the north side of the lake, and into the back roads of Oklahoma. Eventually we approached a large home that was situated right on the water. It looked like something out of a fairy tale, close to a castle. It was mostly white granite block and lacked only a drawbridge to make it at home in the mountains of Europe. A spectacular white granite block wall surrounded the entire grounds.

The grounds were well lit, but the house itself looked deserted. We passed through the gate, parked near the front door, and dismounted.

I catch my breath as Cat removes the jacket, hands it to me, and stands proudly in front of me. There are prettier women…at least by society's definition of beauty. Pick up any magazine and you will find a picture of one. But beauty is as much an attitude as a look, as much a presence as a body type. Cat was sensual, pretty, and alive. She was so, because she *knew* she was. And that makes all the difference.

She moves forward. Embraces me, standing on her tiptoes, her cheek touching mine and her mouth near my ear. "Thank you Dan-ie-yel," she whispers, "you cannot know how much this has meant to me."

I find that I am trembling. She knows my desire.

"Come in if you would like." She whispers. "It would be my honor and pleasure."

I stand frozen. My voice seems to catch in my throat. I roughly whisper, "Cat…I want to…I need to…but…"

She finishes my sentence, "But you cannot. I know. You are a man of honor, and have other commitments."

I draw upon strength from a place I did not previously know existed.

"Yes." The word barely escapes my lips.

Again, placed in my exact situation, with my honor and commitments, there is not a red-blooded male…no real man on the planet…that could have done otherwise. Sometimes honor sucks.

She kisses my cheek and backs away. "We will meet again Dan-ie-yel. When the time is right and we need each other again, we will meet."

She turns and enters the house.

I sigh, take a deep breath, and mount up. I am still trembling. I shrug and turn around and head down the driveway. As I approach the gate a lady with dark hair and smoldering dark eyes steps out from behind the wall. She is clad in a t-shirt, jeans and a leather jacket. I get the immediate impression that she can be very dangerous should the occasion warrant.

I halt the bike and remove my helmet. She stretches up and kisses me on the cheek. "Dan-ie-yel," same accent, "you have brought Cat home. For that we thank you. She has come a very long way."

Curiosity finally starts to get the better of me. "Why was she out there? What happened?"

The dark-haired girl grinned. "She was out there because you needed her. She was out there because she needed you."

Well of course. That explained everything. *Yeah right.*

"I do not understand."

"It is a very wide world Dan-ie-yel. Trust in it."

"I still do not understand."

She looks at me for a moment appraising, probing. Nods. She is kind of peering at me sideways. It suddenly strikes me that she and Cat are related. It is evident in her eyes and her bearing.

She takes my hand, "To paraphrase Shakespeare—'There are more things in Heaven and Earth Dan-ie-yel, then are dreamt of in your philosophy.'"

I still really did not understand, but somehow it didn't matter. "Will she be all right?"

Still smiling, the dark haired girl nods. "She is fine. And you two will meet again." She steps back away from the bike. "Have a nice life Dan-ie-yel." With that she heads toward the house.

I put on my helmet and zip up my jacket against the suddenly falling temperature. As I head for home I mutter, "Miles to go before I sleep."

As I rocket down the highway and into the night, I note how lifted my spirit is. How good I feel. How ready I am for whatever comes along. The world is wide, magical, and interesting. I am very glad to be involved in it.

I had thought I was helping Cat. Maybe she was really helping me. Maybe the dark-haired girl was right, we were helping each other.

Maybe someday I would understand.

I arrived home, surprised my wife with a particularly strong "I love you" and a particularly intense episode of lovemaking, then fell into a deep sleep.

For those skeptics out there, I was ready to dismiss the entire trip as the dream of an over strained and tired mind. I would have except for two things. My uplifted attitude and revived spirit are sustained to this day, and there is the small matter of the card I found weeks later in my jacket pocket.

It was dark red; the same color as Cat's hair, with a single cat's eye, a green one, printed in startling vivid color on the red. On the back is a message:

Daniel, the honor was mine. When the time is right, and we are both ready, we will meet again. Love, Cat

Yes there is a certain magic to the Valkyrie. I like to believe that they attract naked women.

Sigh.

Bonkers?

As if it took anything else to do it, but I think that I have again convinced my wife I am completely insane.

Those that know me are aware that for 20+ years I have been riding, and all that time I have ridden other people's junk, buying older, well-used bikes and slowly resurrecting them from the previous owner's neglect or incompetence. "Well Oiled Machine," my 1980 XS-1100 Midnight Special, was a good example. I spent well over a year restoring her to her former glory.

For all that time (20+ years) I have been wistfully eyeing new bikes and proclaiming, "Someday."

Last fall I woke up one day and discovered that I was no closer to "Someday" than I was 20 years ago. Prices and interest rates were extremely attractive, so I went out and bought the Valkyrie—the exact bike I wanted.

I cannot believe that I waited so long. Nicknamed "The Dragon", no bike has ever fit me so well in size, personality, and temperament. I *ride* other machines; I *become* "The Dragon".

I ride everywhere I can, but am also gearing up for a week or two tour of "out there" this summer. Colorado, New Mexico...who knows? Just going...

I would have been comfortable doing the tour "bone stock" but as I have extensive long riding experience, decided some modifications were in order:

- Saddle bags (to hold stuff).

- Handlebar risers (to position the handlebars a little higher and a little back...I am a big guy)

- Communications gear of some sort…a friend is going with me on "Bunnie", his 1981 Goldwing. Could help to be able to talk.

- Electronic cruise control. That throttle hand can get tired.

- Light bar. Extra lights will help me actually see the local wildlife just *before* impact.

The saddlebags were easy. I had some nice ones that fit perfectly on the bike (and match its lines). I only needed to purchase the stand-offs that keep the bags out of the back tire. A trip to the local bike shop took care of that, and they actually had them in stock!

The handlebar risers were a little bit of a pain, but done in a few hours nonetheless. The bike fits me perfectly now.

The communication's gear was a little more complicated. I installed a CB radio, with audio input so I could play my music into the same headphones in my helmet.

As for the electronic cruise control, I have always done tons of long-distance riding and this is something I have wanted for years. Electronic cruise control for a motorcycle is usually quite expensive, so to save money, I elected to install a universal cruise control that was made to fit a variety of cars and trucks.

So what convinced (again) my wife that I am bonkers? Well…she is familiar with my passion for motorcycles and riding. She also knows how hard I have worked, and the dues I have paid, and how much I really needed the Valkyrie.

So she wanders into the garage to hand me a glass of iced tea (what a woman!) and finds me installing the cruise on "The Dragon".

This required removal of the seat, side-covers, various other covers, the tank, and the air-box. Since I am also installing the light bar, I have the windshield and front turn-signals removed.

Basically "The Dragon" is in small pieces scattered all over the garage. I was sitting in the middle of a blanket covered with various tools, neatly laid out bolts and fittings, and various bits of wire, connectors, linkages, and other cruise control bits. There are partially installed wiring harnesses and controls hanging off parts of the Valkyrie.

You should have seen her face…stunned is an understatement.

For a few moments her mouth worked…she seemingly could not get anything out. Kind of a gag reflex.

She finally manages to get it out, "I can't believe you took apart 'The Dragon'!"

She was not angry or anything…just could not believe it.

My reply? Well…<insert best puppy-dog downcast eyes and solemn/serious look here>, "But I have had it for 4 months already."

She bursts out laughing, shakes her head, and wanders back into the house mumbling something about men.

Days later I finally realize I have neglected to tell her what I was up to. I think she figures I took it apart, just to take it apart.

Why Ride?

"Why do you ride?"

The question was uttered somewhat shyly by the cute gal at "Cavander's Boot City" as she was helping me select a new pair of work/riding boots. I must admit, it took me aback somewhat, for a couple of reasons:

The first reason is that she had spotted me as a rider immediately, and I had tentatively pegged her as one also, even though we had not yet said anything more than, "hello." So…she is a rider…why is she asking the question? Riders *know*, or they do not ride, at least not for long.

Then my brain really grabbed hold of the question. It chewed on it a moment, analyzed it, informed me that it definitely knew the answer, calculated, referenced, imaged, booked additional "left brain" processing time, shuttled, condensed, expanded, distilled, put the whole thing to music, pondered it some more, then it firmly refused to answer.

When I insisted, I pretty much got static, followed by a total reset. I was then forced into a completely involuntary look at the gal again and an enthusiastic, *Hey, she's really cute!* from my brain. I think it was just trying to distract me. Given the…ur…"priorities" of the male brain this usually works, but this time the "priority" was balanced against deep thinking about riding. Great, now I was confused *and* horny. She really was cute. What a piece of work the male brain is…

The main reason the question stumped me was because although I know the answer, and indeed know it to the depths of my soul, I have never attempted to articulate it. It is not something easily put into words.

As I struggled with the concept for a moment, apparently with my mouth hanging open and a far-away look in my eyes, she chuckled and told me she had no easy answer either…but she was hoping somebody would be able to express it someday. According to her, anybody that has ever been able to give her a convenient answer was really not a rider at all. Maybe they own a bike, but simply owning a bike does not make a person a rider.

I concluded my boot purchase, mounted up on the big cruiser, and roared down the highway. Man I love that Valkyrie! As I worked the big machine through the various hazards associated with weekend traffic on the freeways around here, I could not get the question out of my mind. Miles later I was still thinking about it. I was thinking about it so hard, that I abandoned my planned destination completely. I stopped when the batteries in my mp3 player expired and I had to change them. I am not sure where exactly I ended up, but it was pretty there. Ate an ice cream cone, gassed up "The Dragon" and headed for the highway. A sign read "Dallas-93 miles". Hmmmm. I had come just a bit out of my way. Good day.

Riding. It is as necessary to me as breathing. It is a requirement of mind and soul. How to explain it to someone else?

I finally begin to understand that it cannot be explained in a sentence or two. It is far too deep, integral to my being, and plumbed into depths rarely explored. I think the easiest way to explain it is to get the non-rider riding. If after a time, they catch the bug, you can simply say, "See what I mean?" If they do not, then you probably will never cause them to understand.

But then curiosity looms. What about other riders?

Is "why I ride" the same thing as "why you ride"? Probably not exactly. But is it even close? There is no way to tell until we manage to express it somehow. So I am back to my original challenge. Answer a simple question. When I begin to ferret it out, I find myself amazed at how deep it really goes, and exactly what it is firmly attached to.

The beginnings of the answer lie deep within life itself.

There are times that I am really alive, not just surviving. There are times that it all operates in harmony…blood, bone, muscle, mind, soul, and the world all come together to…well…*sing* life and experience.

Those moments are intense and in today's world, with its stresses and pressures, are not always easy to achieve. There is a marked difference between *surviving* and *living*.

For me, finding these moments is easy. There are a few activities that take me out of "surviving" and place me—heart, soul, passion, and mind—squarely and solidly into "living". For these times, there is never any question why I am here, or where life is taking me. During these activities, I *know*.

I am alive. I am a unique combination of blood, bone, muscle, experience, sexuality, and passion. I am proud of what and who I am, even though I do not always know what that is. I revel in life and experience…I am alive…I live…I know.

I know this the most when I am making love, riding, skiing, flying (I am a Cessna pilot), listening to music, and sailing, fast and far.

There really is no order or preference there, and any combination intensifies the "living" (no suggestive comments needed here, trust me, I have already thought of them all).

But again, how to answer the question?

I can answer by listing the things that riding does for me. Where it takes me, what it does for my soul, but that is not the complete answer either. While true, it is unsatisfying, fragmented, and does not provide the complete picture. Is there anything that can?

Finally I decide that in order for someone to understand precisely what riding means to me, they would have to know me, and know me well…maybe one person does, the rest would have to be told somehow.

Again, back to the simple question, "Why do I ride?"

Seems to me that multiple mediums are required to convey the sense of what it is all about.

So here is my do-it-yourself "multi-media presentation". (Note the timely use of trendy "buzz-word")

Combinations of music, experience, and writings are needed if you would understand why I ride.

Writings:

I love to write, and am surprised, thrilled, and flattered when someone enjoys what I have done. If you would know me without actually "knowing," then my writing is a place to start. The motorcycling stories I have written illustrate a little piece at a time what we are talking about here…just a peak into my soul if you will. Maybe they can help you see it too.

Music:

Music is critical to me. It allows me to organize my mind, make sense of the world, express and experience passion, and helps to bring back the ability to see and experience the magic that still exists in the world. I have hundreds of CD's, and my collection spans nearly every genre. I like some of everything, depending on life and my mood at the time. The following songs may or may not be favorites, depending on when you ask me, but they clearly illustrate what I am trying to communicate here…provided that they are used correctly. Instructions follow:

Cram the following songs into your mp3 player:
One Wild Night—Bon Jovi.
Fields of Fire, a Tribute—The Killdares (Live Album).
It's My Life—Bon Jovi.
Don't Walk Away—Pat Benetar.
A New Day Has Come—Celine Dion.
I'm Alive—Celine Dion.
Only the Strong Survive—Reo Speedwagon.
All Fired Up—Pat Benetar.
So Right—Bell Book & Candle.

If you have not heard these, check 'em out, they are worth the effort. Then fill your player to capacity with all the stuff you like.

Experience:

Pick a hot summer night and take off down a lonely road. Drive a couple hundred, or a couple thousand miles with no place in particular in mind. Make sure you have fresh batteries for your mp3 player, and enjoy your music.

When you get home, take some time to reflect. You want to go again, don't you? Hot (or cold), dusty (or wet), wrung out, hungry, weary traveler, and yet you want to go again.

Now you see...now you *know*...that's why I ride. See? Easy.

If you do not have time or interest for all that, if you think you can get an answer without "knowing" then things are much simpler...

Why do I ride?

Because.

Now...Why do you ride?

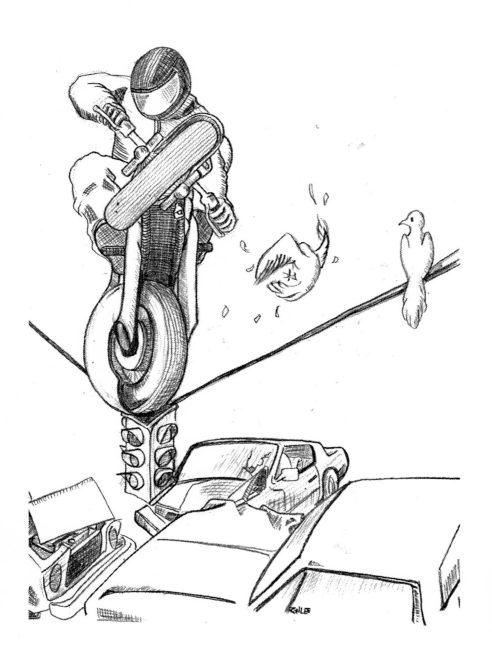

Left Turn Madness

Today as I was headed out on the Valkyrie to pick up some parts for the wife's misbehaving car, I was approaching the stoplight at the intersection near my house. Typical two street intersection, each street 3 lanes in each direction (divided).

I had the green, and was not blocked from view by any leading cars.

Oncoming fast car entered her left turn lane closely followed by two others. They were really moving…probably 20mph over the 40mph speed limit. Although they were slowing, instinct—my little voice basically said, *Oh crap!*—told me the first car was not going to stop and yield the right of way to me. Bummer, since I was proceeding straight through the intersection.

Time slows to a crawl. Icy calm clamps down. Heart rate climbs to unhealthy levels. Adrenalin flows. Massive strength is readily available. I feel I could crush bricks with my bare hands. "The Dragon" and I merge and become one.

This is the classic left turn motorcycle killer, except there was absolutely no obstruction to anyone's vision. These morons are the reason the law requires us to have a headlight on all the time. Fat lot of good that does…people gotta look up every once and a while…

I pulled an extreme braking/evasive trick and ended up stopped in the intersection—kind of right in the middle. "The Dragon" is graceful and responsive under pressure. I am a big and strong guy, and the Valkyrie and I mesh together well. Barely missed the errant car, and the driver was looking at me wide-eyed as she passed by.

Sheesh. Bad enough, but the car following her was blissfully unaware that he should also yield to oncoming traffic that has the green. *Oh crap!* says the little voice again. I am stopped in the exact center of the entire intersection…the place that no car ever occupies if everyone is doing everything right, so I am no longer a factor. There are other cars behind me however…The oncoming turner is apparently fixated on the preceding car and is not paying attention. He barely clears me (I do not think he ever saw me) and creams the car that was passing by me in the center lane through the intersection. Pretty much a head-on…I get heavily sprayed with flying glass and gasoline, and got a very good close up view of the ass end of his car as it "whooshes" by me in an arc spewing gas, but fortunately get missed by all the heavier bits randomly traveling about the intersection. *Brrrrr*…I can still read you his license plate number…it is etched into my brain.

Now I have had enough adventure for one day, but like lemmings over a cliff the third oncoming car also turns left. At least he manages at the last second to notice the carnage in his path, but that is bad for me, as he starts to swing wide to get around the mess and is moving too fast to stop. That puts me square in his sights. Tires are screeching. I can clearly see his face. I know he is going to hit me, he knows he is going to hit me, and he knows that I know that he is going to hit me. This is going to hurt.

I am a small plane pilot, and one of the things I learned in my training, is that you *always* make a decision. Right, wrong, whatever…when things are coming to a lurch *make a decision*—Take action. Anything will be an improvement over the decision that will be made for you if you do not do so.

Also, my Texas upbringing says no matter how hopeless something seems, never, *never*, quit. Basically, never stop driving. Lot's of people freeze when they know the shit is about to hit the fan. What they need to realize is that there are times when nothing you can do can possibly make the situation worse. By definition, that means that anything you do can make the situation better…

So—That's it, I'm outta here…

Wrapped up the RPM's and popped the clutch. Did not really care which direction I took off in...anything was better than what was coming.

ZZZZZAAAAAPPPPPSSSCREACH!!! "The Dragon" roared. Jheeez what a bike! She is a living being...there is no other explanation for the union between the machine and myself. Warp/pop (space time thingy) and suddenly (poof) I am in the parking lot of the McDonalds/ Chevron across the intersection. I remember *nothing* between popping the clutch, and putting my foot down in the parking lot. The car never touched me.

I very carefully shut the Valkyrie off with the kill switch as there was less gas dripping from there than elsewhere. I am praying for no sparks. Now that I was out of danger the adrenaline was exacting its price for the enhanced senses and reactions before, and due to the shakes and weakness I was unable to try to lift my left foot even enough to put the stand down or I would have dropped the bike. It was all I could do for the moment to stand there holding the bike up and breathe. Takes me a good two minutes to clear my vision and moderate the shakes enough to get off the bike. I was wearing a full-face helmet, but had the face shield open as I have a windshield on my Valkyrie and it was gorgeous today. I have glass and gas all over me.

The Calvary has arrived. *Great* ems response times here. They are starting to take care of the mess of the two cars in the intersection. All the other involved parties (first and last turner) bugged out.

Got some paper towels off the gas pump rack and tried to get the glass and gas off me. Nobody using the service station would look at me. I think it was obvious I needed some help. Whatever they are putting in the gas lately, it really *burns* the ur...more sensitive areas of one's anatomy. Not much to do about it at the moment except grimace and curse. Have some very minor scratches on my arms from the glass, but they bled profusely as glass cuts do, and the gas made them sting furiously.

I am sure I was a sight. The occasional expletive forcefully and involuntarily uttered probably shooed some folks off. Some folks are just a bit timid when a 300-pound, adrenalin fired, shaking, bloodied, gasoline soaked biker is stomping around. The toughest thing was that I had glass in my helmet padding around the face, and really needed to pick it out before removing the helmet, but I could not see and to my embarrassment my hands were still shaking.

I honestly can say the shakes were not fear. I am fairly un-phased about the close call, but the high adrenalin kick really does exact a terrible price later…if you have never experienced this it is difficult to describe…suffice it to say that when the adrenalin kicks in, you *will* do something, and when it is over you *will* have a few moments where you are all but incapacitated.

Gasoline is not a good substitute for eye drops, so about the time I manage to see clearly again a police officer approaches to check on me. He helps me get the bigger shards of glass out of the padding around my face and then I can remove my helmet. About this time a rather timid lady hesitantly hands me her bottled water and a napkin. Finally! Somebody with her wits about her. I'd have kissed her full on the mouth if I could have seen her clearly, but instead I thank her profusely and immediately upend the half the bottle of water directly into my open eyes which are by now red and swollen. I use the rest of the water and the napkin to swab my face and eyelids off. What a relief!

The officer had been in the parking lot across the street watching for redlight runners and saw the entire thing. He said he could see exactly what was happening, and was on the radio calling, "Motorcycle rider down!" before the thing was half over with. I was very glad to prove him wrong.

Claims I am the best motorcycle rider he has ever seen. Apparently I wheelied across the intersection threading between other moving cars and entered the parking lot at a very high speed. He said I was moving so fast that he was sure I was going to run the Valkyrie right through the building. That would give a new meaning to "drive through" at the

McDonalds I guess. But to his surprise I stopped under complete control in a very short space. He was really impressed with "The Dragon". So am I.

I would not presume to argue with a police officer (those that know me recognize that as humor)...he can believe I am the best if he wants to...but between us, really I am not the best, I am lucky. To a certain extent, we make our own luck. I do have and hone my riding skills, but nothing I did was planned out in advance. Time had run out for that. Trust in your instincts, skills, faith, and luck. Never quit. *Ever.*

Sheesh.

The two cars were toast, and both drivers went away in the ambulances, but were conscious and walking. Probably not seriously injured.

As for "The Dragon", she got carefully and cheerfully washed and waxed, and we treated ourselves to a 100-mile ride to nowhere in this gorgeous weather. The repairs on the wife's cage could wait.

We have a limited number of days in this world. Let's ride.

Hell and Gone

PROLOGUE

Man oh man...

The night was crisp, clear, calm, and cool. Perfect motorcycling weather—we could not have asked for any better. Under the Texas summer night skies, with the brilliant moon and intense stars, riding is sheer pleasure. We should have stopped to rest hours ago, but could not bring ourselves to interrupt the ride. There is a price to be paid for this however—the journey must come to an end that much sooner. Texas goes on forever, but on a night like this, forever is not nearly far enough.

We smelled Dallas for a couple hours before we reached it. Motorcycling on a clear and cool night really connects you to the world around you. After a few minutes you are intimate with the rush of the wind and the smells, sounds, and essence of life. After several hours, senses are heightened to an unimagined level, and we had been doing this for *days*. We were more a part of the motorcycles we were astride than most can understand...the intricate precision machines having become an extension of our bone, muscle, blood, and awareness. Through them, we knew the road. Through them, we knew the world. Through them, we knew ourselves.

As we approached the city, very few cars shared the space with us on the freeways. Four o'clock in the morning will often have that result.

I spoke to James on the radio, "Hard to believe we are already here."

"Yeah, me too. I'm not ready to quit yet."

Eight days, 3000 miles. Five states, hundreds of towns, dozens of gas stops. Cold, rain, dust, storms, intense heat, blistering sun, smoke, fire, ferocious winds that pounded us unmercifully, and the last 860 miles with only stops for gas and food, and still he had not had enough. I guess I know my friend pretty well.

I chuckled to myself. I had been thinking about the past few days' experience, and enjoying the current leg of the trip. All we had done, the things we had seen, all we had been through. Perspective had certainly shifted. But where had it shifted *to*?

We reached the split where James would continue south to his home, and I peeled off to the east. Just minutes till we arrived. Minutes till it was over. Little was said. There was little to say. We already *knew*.

We had set out on this journey looking for something, we were not really sure what…and we had certainly found something. The question was whether what we found was what we had been seeking.

At the moment I was having trouble answering that question. *Eight days, 3000 miles…*

I was not ready to quit either. Not by a long shot.

INTRODUCTION

"Why am I here?" I asked myself for at least the 10th time in as many minutes. The question was a complicated one. I was not asking why I was in that particular location, I wish it were that simple! I was asking more of why am I forcing myself to do what I am doing. What is my motivation? Where is my passion? I had it before, where had it gone? When had it gone? I could not find an answer for myself...I really could not remember at the moment. Frankly that terrified me.

The purpose of man is to live, not to exist... <Jack London>

I am passionate about life. I find satisfaction and excitement in most things that I do...life is not...well...*alive* otherwise. Lately life has become dead with trivial tasks and other people's problems consuming so much of my time, creativity, and effort, that all the things that I am passionate about have been squeezed completely out of my life. When I begin to squirm, to attempt to get back some of the things that matter to me, the things that define my *self,* suddenly the people I love and respect think I am a selfish bastard.

Am I doomed to live the dead life?

I gazed in bewilderment at the many computer monitors surrounding my desk. The problems I had been working on, the ones that had seemed so critical just a few moments ago, had not gone away, they just somehow did not matter anymore. Mechanically I began to clear the backlogs and fix the bugs that had to be corrected before I could leave for the day. I do my job, and do it well, but internal conflict and confusion, *unease*, reigned today.

Why am I here?

Spurts of lucidity, surrounded by vast periods of functioning strictly mechanically. Passionlessly carrying out my obligations. This had been going on for days, maybe months. I am not sure when I first became aware of it.

Remember who you are…

It was beginning to become clear to me that I had to do something. Change something, or I was going to lose my "self". This is not a new problem; countless men have succumbed to this before me. Indeed, I myself have experienced it to some degree before. This time however, I somehow know that it is absolutely critical. A juxtaposition has been reached. Passion defines my soul, infuses my being. It is a part of who I am, of what I can become. To lose it would destroy me.

I have been here before, lost it before. This time is different. Like a drowning man, there are only so many times that you can struggle to the surface. Losing it this time will cost me my "self", my love of life, and my perception of the magic that is in the world. Attempts to articulate the problem, worry, and unease to the people I love have been met with a laugh and "Midlife crisis," or a similar comment. Call it what you will, trivialize it if you must, but that does not reduce its severity, its validity, or its impact.

I've got to get out of here.

Guess I am not quite as domesticated as I am supposed to be. The vague dissatisfaction with the progress and arrangement of my life was starting to become focused, more important. I was beginning to understand that the overwhelming yet somehow trivial obligations had sidelined relationships with the people that I care for. As I slowly sacrificed the quality of my time and the passion in the relationships with my wife, my self, and my friends to the ever-increasing commitments and obligations, I began to be aware of just how wrong this was, regardless of how many men have come this way before me. How far does this have to go?

In a world full of fugitives, the person taking the opposite direction will appear to be running away... <T. S. Eliot>

Suddenly I felt the need to visit my best friend. I have known James for well over 20 years, 20 was a while ago, and was when we stopped counting, and in many ways our lives have run parallel. I would trust James with my life, and if anybody on the planet understands even a part of me, it is he.

When did the road I chose to travel, become the one that I am on?

We rarely see each other nowadays. Work, family, and other obligations have even consumed that ability too.

Lost......I'm lost...

I managed to steal a few minutes and went to see him. I wanted to talk to him about my unease...see if I could at least make him understand. Turns out it was unnecessary. I could see it in his eyes, read it in his demeanor. Words were not truly necessary. Once again, somehow, he was in the same boat as I.

I am frightened of this thing that I've become...

Suddenly it was clear to me that there was a path that could help me regain my perspective, charge up my soul. Maybe I would could even spend some time thinking and establish an equilibrium between the demands imposed by *living*, and the demands required to *live*.

If life is a road, then the soul is a motorcycle...

James and I have been riding together as long as we have known each other. Riding settles the mind, crystallizes your thinking, recharges the soul, and puts life itself in perspective.

I looked sharply at James and uttered two words, "Road trip?"

"Yeah…yeah."

"Where to?" I muttered, not really caring. The destination is just the excuse.

"Not sure. Just gone. Really gone."

"Yeah," I stated. "Hell and gone!"

Something was lost. Something was missing. It was time to go on the offensive. It was time to take it back.

And so was born "Hell and Gone"…

THE NIGHT BEFORE

Where the Hell Are We Going?

"Hell and Gone" was conceived as a 10-day motorcycle road trip. The 10-day block was selected as that is a typical block of vacation days that we could get off based on our respective schedules. A last minute (but typical) bit of confusion at work cut us short by a day and some, so 8-days it became.

I would be traveling on my Valkyrie, and James on his Gold Wing. We figured somewhere west, mountains, open spaces. Motorcycle-riding places. Deserts too, man and machine needed testing. Colorado, New Mexico, Utah, and Arizona immediately came to mind.

Finally James said, "How about the Grand Canyon?"

"Sure, but let's go for the North Rim." The North Rim is more remote, and a little more difficult to get to. 8-days to get to and back from the Grand Canyon. This would leave lots of time for seeing other sights, taking detours, riding, and *living*.

Now understand, the Grand Canyon was not our destination, it was an arbitrary turn-around point. Basically it was selected to give us a direction. Remember, the destination is only the excuse.

The Phantom Socks:

Just before "Hell and Gone" was to start, my wife had left on a two-week trip to visit family in North Carolina. Between getting her ready for her trip, getting her on the plane, and a frantic last few days at work, I found myself alone—except for our two cats—and packing late the night before James and I were to leave. Normally I do not prepare for a 8-day motorcycle trip 8 hours before we are to leave, and normally do not spend the last night alone. Not quite the send-off I was hoping for. Life often throws interesting twists.

Roll with the changes.

Any long-distance rider can tell you that there are a few things that are vitally important to a successful trip. Clean and plentiful socks and underwear top this list. I was laying out stuff to pack in my duffel bag. I had placed some clothes in the duffel, but had the socks (rolled up in "sock balls") stacked on the bed beside the duffel. The phone rang, and in my typical male distracted way I had lost the handset and had to search to answer it. It was a salesman, of course. It was 10:30pm. Don't these guys ever quit?

I finally located the handset, "Hello?"

"Is the lady of the house there?

"Well, yeah, but she is locked in the closet right now. She is only allowed out on Saturday between three and four o'clock. Can I take a message?"

"urrrr......" Click. Buzzzzzz.

Salesman, will they ever learn?

Anyway, returning to my packing, all my socks were gone from the bed. I did not remember packing them, but again, I am a guy. My wife says I can hide my own Easter eggs, and she is probably right! I finished up the packing, but I could not stop thinking about the socks. They are so important that my brain just would not turn loose of the question. I did not remember packing them, but could clearly remember everything else.

Dug through the duffel and they were not in there. Ten sock-balls were missing. *Sheesh*. Glad I checked. Must have carried them with me when I went to answer the phone. Proceeded to search the house, but could find no sign of them. Retraced my steps several times, noticed I had scarfed a Diet-Coke in there somewhere, so I even checked the refrigerator.

Only a guy would wind up looking in the refrigerator for his socks. No luck.

What the heck?

I had searched for the socks for about half an hour and found no trace. How can you lose ten sock-balls? My wife is always teasing me that I cannot ever find anything in our house, but ten sock-balls? I even looked in the garage!

Gave up and dug through my sock drawer again. Found five more pair and set them on the bed. Five pair was not enough, and some of them were a bit scruffy. It was getting late, and now I was facing a trip to the 24-hour Wal-Mart to get some more. Frustrating. The wife will never let me hear the end of this. Grabbed my wallet off the coffee table, and then had to grab my keys from the bedroom. I gave a quick glance at the three sock balls left on the bed.

Wait a minute…There were only three sock balls left on the bed!

Urrrrr…?

While I stood there pondering the situation a moment, I heard a soft "clunk" from the guest bathroom. I wandered down the hall and poked my head around the corner and peered in the bathroom door.

SHWOOOOOSH! I was run down by one of our cats. I was nearly bowled over, and practically jumped out of my shoes. Glad I was not armed at that moment, there would have been bullet holes all over the house.

Those that doubt that you can be run down by a cat have not met "Casper", our 22-pound Maine Coon cat. He is a big sweetie, but he is large and strong. He is also very fast; you know it when he gallops by, especially if you turn out to be a hazard to his navigation.

Now what was he up to? Both the cats had been behaving strangely since the wife left. Basically they were pissed about it and figured it was my fault. Cats are very expressive, and I had no trouble at all understanding that. As soon as I started packing they were positively frantic—at least as frantic as you can get if you are one of nature's most laid-back and relaxed (and lazy) creatures.

I turned on the light in the guest bathroom. Nothing was out of place. But I had heard a "clunk". What could be up? I opened the cabinet under the sink and behold! Twelve sock balls began spilling out. Mystery solved! Cats are weird. Well, I guess we knew that already.

I gathered the socks up and headed back down the hall. I met Casper mid-hall, head held high and proudly carrying the remaining three sock-balls. Busted! He managed to look very guilty yet elated at the same time, and gave me a look that clearly said, "You'll never find these!" He then turned tail, and vanished. The three sock-balls are still MIA.

The main thought besides *Cats are weird* in my mind was that I am really glad I found the socks. My wife is already pretty sure I am nuts, and she would have eventually been the one to find all the missing socks under the cabinet. I can imagine her asking, "What the heck did you put them down there for?" And of course I would have no idea what she was talking about (as usual).

Traveling Light?

I finally finished packing and began piling all the stuff on the bike. I drive a 2001 Valkyrie Standard, and as such, she does not have all the bags all over the place that most touring bikes have. (And I like it like that!). I have a set of soft, leather-like saddlebags that I use when I travel. I also can bungee an incredible amount of stuff in duffels on the back seat.

The right saddlebag contained: My toolkit, large fluffy towel—very important, it's a dangerous universe, don't get caught without your towel—a spray can of Lemon Pledge for cleaning windshields and helmet visors, and a rag for using with the Pledge.

Lemon Pledge is an old biker's trick. It cleans bugs and dust off windshields/visors very easily, and makes it easier to clean the next time. It also has the added benefit of causing water to bead up and blow off your windshield and visor if (when) you get caught in the rain.

The left saddlebag contained my sneakers, as I wear boots while actually riding. It also contained my tinted helmet visor which is indispensable if you are heading for several days in the desert. For my helmet I also carried spare visor pivots—the hinges the face shield pivots on—as they are prone to breakage. That left a bit of room to stuff anything needed or acquired along the way.

I then bungeed several duffels on the back seat, starting with the widest/largest and working my way up. The duffels were black water-proofed canvas duffels. They are not expensive and keep the gear clean and dry.

The bottom one contained my sleeping bag, and my laptop in its own neoprene zippered sleeve. I did not really have to carry the laptop but chose to as it did not take much room, and it could be useful for unloading the memory cards for the digital camera should I manage to fill them up. Might be fun to preview our pictures in the evening as well. I intended to take a lot of pictures on this trip. Maybe I would feel like writing too. It was also there in case work needed me and actually somehow managed to get in touch with me. Many of the more pricey chain hotels have broadband Internet access, and I can also dial in from any phone and troubleshoot most problems. I was not expecting any. But such is the nature of my job. We have back-up plans for our back-up plans.

The next duffel up contained my tent and ground cloth. Could have fit them in with the sleeping bag, but it takes no extra room to put them in a separate duffel, is easier, and keeps the sleeping bag cleaner. In case you are wondering, the tent did come with its own case, but once opened, I could never get it to fit back in the dratted thing. The machine that stuffs that tent in the case at the factory must be amazing! They are stuffed in there so tight that one day one of those tents is going to reach critical mass and explode in transit. The duffel was easy and cheap.

The next duffel contained all my clothes, including the previously cat-napped socks. The top and smallest duffel contained all my riding gear; rain-suit, maps, sunscreen, sunglasses, Deep Woods Off (34% deet, woohoo!), the digital camera, extra CD's and batteries for my camera and mp3 player, and anything else that I might need to get at fairly easily.

Ready to go!

I wearily showered, warily glanced at the cats (Casper was acting like nothing at all had happened) turned out the lights, and went to bed to try to get a couple hours sleep. James was due in the morning at 5:00am.

DAY ONE

Let's Get the Hell Out of Here!

Finally the morning of our departure arrived. We were figuring on a 500-mile day through West Texas, so an early "scram" was called for. Riding in the west Texas heat for extended periods can be somewhat taxing, and we were planning for a significant portion of our trip to be in those conditions. An early start would help in that hopefully we would not be overly frying ourselves on the first leg of the trip.

Did you know there is actually such a thing as 4:30 in the morning? Ahhhcccckkk. I was feeling a little guilty for actually getting a couple hours sleep, as due to the scheduling snafu at work, James had worked the previous night, then had to pack up. He would get no sleep at all!

James arrived, and we finished final preparations on the bikes. I quickly snapped a picture of my odometer so I could remember the starting mileage. If I just wrote it down, I would undoubtedly lose the paper I wrote it on. Even though I am a guy, I am unlikely to lose the digital camera or the laptop.

I took a sweep through the house to make sure I had left nothing on. The phone rang. *Uh Oh*...a phone call at 5:00am. That cannot be good.

I hunted down the handset, "Hello?"

"Is the lady or the man of the house there?"

Another salesman. I have never bought anything, ever, on a cold call. Will these guys ever quit? And why the hell are they calling at a 5:00am on a Saturday?

"Well, which do you want, the lady or the man?"

"Um...the lady I guess."

"Sorry. The lady of the house is unavailable at the moment."

"Well, the man then."

"That would be me, but I have no time to talk right now. See, I just stuffed the lady of the house down the disposal, I think my neighbor heard all the screaming, and now I have to flee the country. Bye." As I hung up the phone I was mumbling, "Mexico…yeah…Mexico sounds good…" loud enough for him to hear me.

It occurred to me sometime after we departed that my friend Mike (hi Mike) would be stopping by to take care of the cats, I hope the cops are not waiting for him with some really odd questions when he arrives…

Gone!

We departed at about 5:30am on Saturday, June the 15th into unseasonably cool weather. I know we Texans talk about our highly variable weather so much as to be cliché, but today was a typical example. We were to be chilled, roasted, chilled again, rained on, blown around, and flat plastered by a 75-mile long dust storm with 60 mph crosswinds today. All that was to be before we left Texas.

A quick stop at the corner 7–11 to gas up the bikes and replenish James's cigar supply, and we were on the road. It is almost worth it to get up at 5:00am on a Saturday morning just to get a chance to drive on the Dallas freeways sans traffic. What a difference! For those of you that do not live here, I can only say, that there is no good way to get from anywhere to anyplace in the Dallas metro area during the day. The freeways carry as much as 200% more vehicles than they were designed to handle, construction is constant, and the mass-transit system is an expensive joke, as it usually takes longer than the clogged freeways and side streets. The result is a frustrating mess in an otherwise very interesting city.

Our plan was to avoid the super-slabs for the most part on this trip. The first leg was to be Dallas to Carlsbad, New Mexico, about 500 miles. We headed out of Dallas on Interstate-20, correctly figuring that the traffic would be easy this time of day, and it was the fastest way to get us out of the metro area. Again, the city here is massive…we were nearly 75 miles into the trip before we were truly out of the congestion.

We split off of Interstate-20 onto US 180 at Weatherford. This would take us the rest of the way to Carlsbad, with only stops for gas and drinks. US 180 is an interesting and motorcycle friendly road. It is in good condition for the most part and is not heavily traveled as it parallels Interstate-20 and most folks and the trucks use that instead. It has a 70 mph speed limit except in the towns, and plenty of gas/lunch/coke stops. The scenery is varied, and the people in the towns are interesting and generally friendly.

Watch out for the chicken fried steaks however…

The temperature had been comfortable in the DFW area, but it dropped by 10 degrees or so as we cleared the cities. At Mineral Wells, our first gas stop, we were downright cold and debated breaking out the jackets. But the sun was now turning up the intensity and we expected the temperature to rise rapidly. We were correct. Over the next 2 stops or so we began to roast. Typical Texas.

Suddenly, the temperature again plummeted as we approached a massive line of thunderstorms. We were treated to gorgeous views, with the road winding away into the distance, and the hostile sky growling overhead. Vivid, startling beams of sunlight occasionally burning through the clouds lit the scenery with an eerie surreal glow.

The road seemed exceptionally friendly, obligingly winding around between the big boomers, and missing the downpours. It frequently cut right through the bright beams of sunlight. Lightning on the horizon kept time with the music on the mp3 player. Gorgeous riding. We debated several times over the radio whether it was time to stop and don the rain gear, but cresting each rise would reveal the road taking another twist between the storms, sparing us the showers.

That is of course, until the last hill. We crested the hill and suddenly found ourselves in a heavy downpour. There was no real convenient place to stop and put on the gear, under a bridge is usually nice, but there were none available as the roads do not cross very often out here. We stopped beside the road and got wetter even as we donned the gear.

I found much to my irritation that I could not put on my water-proof riding gloves. My hands were slightly wet, and that caused them to stick immediately to the lining of the gloves. They cannot be put on if your hands are even slightly damp. Useless things, but now I know.

We continued on (me sans gloves) and naturally, the universal law of motorcycles and rain gear manifested itself. Basically this means that as soon as the time and trouble are taken to stop and don the rain gear, the rain will stop.

It stopped within 5 miles, basically when we crested the next hill we encountered one of those typical Texas weather changes. We were suddenly and completely out of the cloud cover and into intense sunlight. It was time for the extra-crispy baking action of the West Texas hot winds to kick in. We were 20 miles or so from our next gas stop, so we continued on and removed the gear at the next stop. This was the last time the rain gear was needed on this trip, and means that I wore it for more miles on dry pavement than I did in the rain. Just the way a trip is supposed to be.

As we removed the bone-dry hot wind baked rain-gear, exposing the mildly damp persons underneath, James with his typical talent for stating the obvious said, "Maybe one day we will learn—stop and put on the rain gear, *before* we get wet."

We have been doing this for something over 20 years. Not sure that there is any hope that we will ever learn the lesson.

I wish I could say for sure what town we were in, because I need to warn you about the chicken fried steak (CFS). We both ordered it as the waitress had said, "Can't go wrong." when asked about it. *Urrg.* This was another one of those that will stick with you for a couple hundred miles, and has you heading for the restroom before you even finish it. Tasted pretty good though, so gave no real early warning about its intentions. *not* a good thing on a long-distance motorcycle trip. It does not get the "Worst in Texas" title, that is still held by the CFS we encountered in Falfurrias, Texas during our trip to the SPI Bike Fest.

We survived the encounter, barely. What does not kill you makes you stronger, yes? Maybe we can build up an immunity, or develop a vaccine.

We later encountered another one of these "Stealth Chicken Fried Steaks" (SCFS) in Roswell, New Mexico. A SCFS tastes all right but whammies you mercilessly later, and we have identified a common trait, kind of an early warning system. Basically, if they bring out the CFS and it is floating on top of the gravy instead of covered in it, that is a bad sign. Possible SCFS. Beware.

Dust In the Wind...

Leaving town, we were in typical Texas summer conditions. Hot, windy, sunny, and the intense blue sky goes on from horizon to horizon. Gorgeous. A few miles down the road we topped another hill and found a strange sight indeed...the sky at the horizon was distinctly orange. Rather startling really, it contrasted amazingly with the intense blue. It was not an atmospheric illusion, as horizon in the other three directions appeared normal.

We finally decided it was smoke or dust, but were having difficulty comprehending the scale of it. For quite some time it stayed on the horizon as we were traveling toward it at 75 mph or so, thus slowly but steadily revealing its scale to minds that still could not quite accept it.

Turned out it was a dust storm. A big one. As we approached I commented to James on the radio that there must be a hell of a lot of wind in there. It was fairly calm where we were at the moment. There had to be some sort of dry-line or convergence of pressure systems there. A violent one. The thunderstorms we drove through earlier were what are called "outflow boundaries" from the collision of these two systems. Shock waves essentially, a hundred miles away. Nature is incredible. Despite years of this kind of experience, I still never quite grasp the *scale* of it all.

Eventually we entered the storm, and I was correct about the wind. *Wham!* We went from fairly calm conditions to 60–70 mph south winds. This, of course was to be nearly direct crosswinds for us as we were headed west. *Sheesh*. The dust was bright orange, and was a result of these massive winds over hundreds of square miles of freshly plowed cotton fields. The dirt is bright orange too! It does *not* taste like chicken.

Cotton really is king out here. Hundreds of very large fields—literally thousands of square miles worth—those huge sprinklers that walk around in gigantic circles, and cotton harvesting equipment make for an interesting and varied view. The occasional cotton gin and grain storage facility, sometimes only feet from the roads, created windbreaks that buffeted the bikes violently in the transitions. Whoosh, *bang!* Challenging riding indeed.

I expect the dust storm was hundreds of miles long, blowing tons of sandy dirt northward. It was at least 75 miles wide, we had to cross it. That was the width of the area that had all the plowed fields. We exited the storm when we left the area of plowed fields, but did not leave the violent winds until we reached Carlsbad. They were so intense that our necks ached from keeping our heads straight against the side pressure of the wind.

The last hundred miles of the trip were amazingly hot. In west Texas, we had encountered some heat, but shortly after we entered New Mexico we were assaulted by extremely hot winds out of the desert. It would get hotter in massive jumps, suddenly hitting you with a hot wind that felt like it sucked the breath out of you for a moment. The temperature would rise about 10 degrees in a jump. We were panting as we approached Carlsbad. It was 114 degrees.

The crosswinds and the heat seriously impacted our fuel mileage too. My bike will normally go about 120 miles before I have to switch to reserve. James' bike will normally go about 116 miles, then he is out, as his reserve does not function. Not counting my reserve, our range is virtually identical.

As we approached Carlsbad I was showing about 90 miles since the last fuel stop. We had just entered the outskirts of town when "The

Dragon" lost power. *What the?* Oops. Switched her to reserve and she came right back.

If I was out of gas, James would soon follow. The difference is I can drive another 50 miles or so on reserve. James has to push.

I keyed up the radio, "Hey dude, I'm out," and then in my typical supportive lifelong friend role I added, "and you're screwed."

"Yeah, I know. I have a gauge remember?" That is typical, classic James. Aware of the problem, but since there was nothing to be done—there are no stations, or anything else for that matter, outside of Carlsbad—there was no sense complaining or commenting about it.

The Gold Wing has a gas gauge, and for some strange reason it is remarkably accurate. When the needle hits the red area, you must change to reserve. If you are James, you are out of luck. Red means you are out of gas. We did not want to push a Gold Wing in this heat.

So, now we needed the first gas station we can find. Unfortunately Carlsbad is under construction. Since we critically need gas, naturally the first three stations we passed could not be reached from our side of the road due to the construction. Finally we approached one we could get to. The Gold Wing ran out of gas literally feet short of the pump. Life is good sometimes.

We grabbed a hotel room at the Motel 6, turned the AC in the room on "deep chill", and unloaded the bikes.

We met a man that was in Hell there.

While we were unloading the bikes a full mini-van pulled up. It was a classic stereotype of the haggard American family on the vacation from hell. The driver was the husband, and he was patiently enduring four screaming kids throwing things around the car, and an equally noisy (and downright mean) wife screaming at him. Toys and soda bottles spilled out when the door was opened. The wife went in to get a hotel room.

The man sat behind the wheel with his head in his hands. As I was looking at him, he slowly raised his head and looked over at us. You could see it in his eyes. His story was plain. He had once had a bike and had given it up for his wife. If you are a rider (not just a bike owner) giving up your bike is much like cutting off a piece of your soul. It simply cannot be done without doing more damage than good. He had done it, and right now he could not remember why. He envied us. He wanted to chuck it all. I expect that a word or two of encouragement from us and he would have. We could have pulled him out. We did not. Still not sure if we did the right thing. The prisons we sometimes build for ourselves can be the cruelest ones of all, perhaps more so because we know that we and we alone hold all the keys.

We finished unloading the bikes, and headed out for dinner. Pot roast and mashed potatoes for James, and breakfast Dagwood (ham, cheese, bacon, eggs on a bun) for me. Hot fudge sundaes for dessert.

The AC at the hotel was loudly protesting its burden and rattling intensely, but it was cooling so we wedged pieces of hotel stuff into the cracks in the metal covers to shut it up.

James had not had any sleep in something like 40 hours; I had managed 4 hours in the last 40, so we snapped off the lights, and were asleep before the light faded away…

Faster than the speed of dark.

DAY TWO

KaWhump!

Day two started with a bang, or at least a protracted thump that brought me instantly awake. Not the usual doors closing and people tromping up and down the stairs that you always hear at a hotel, but a heavy "thump" right there in the room, and vibration that rattled the floor.

I awoke alert, and due to a lot of world experience quickly dismissed the possibility of any immediate threat. We were not on fire, we were not drowning, and nobody is stupid enough to irritate a Texan sleeping in his hotel room…much less two of them. I lay there a minute, in a heightened state of alertness, figuring it would resolve itself soon enough. Shortly the compressor in the air-conditioning unit kicked back on with a laborious whine, and a tremendous vibrating rumble.

Ah. What had awakened me was the poor thing finally but temporarily catching up with its burden and shutting down for a moment. The unit was really on its last legs. Some of the hotel stuff we had wedged into the cracks in the metal covers to shut up the vibration had also worked loose. The most effective piece, the TV channel guide, was laying on the floor.

Our motel room did not have an alarm clock so I wondered about the time. Light leaking around the heavy curtains was indeterminate, as the parking lot was well lit. We had left a wake up call for 6am, as I had forgotten my travel alarm in the frenzy of last minute packing. Surely we could count on getting the call…

Long dependence on alarm clocks to get this sleep deprived soul to work on time—at a job that is *all* deadlines—has instilled an almost irrational attention to the time that I had not yet managed to shed on this trip. Finally curiosity and uncertainty got the better of me. I fumbled around a bit and grabbed my pager (the only clock I carry on my person) and thumbed the button. Two minutes of blinking, some extremely blurry numbers, and a hasty calculation of the time zone difference determined that it was 6:40am. They had missed the wake-up call.

We wanted to get an early start, so we could have a leisurely breakfast before we went to saunter around the Caverns for a while. We were then heading up through Roswell and then west toward Arizona. An early start was important to avoid the heat.

I looked at the misshapen lump in the next bed. "James...hey...wake up. They missed the wake-up call."

We were up, showered, packed, and ready in record time. As we were getting ready to leave the phone rang. It was the 6am wake-up call. They got it right, I had misread the pager. Sigh. At least we got our early start! This was the point when I was finally able to shed the "deadline orientation" that I had been stuck in. What did it matter? We would get there when we got there.

Had a very leisurely breakfast at Denny's. We were eating like pigs; I had iced tea, eggs, bacon, sausage, ham, and pancakes. Yum.

That's a Damn Big Hole in the Ground.

The road to the Carlsbad Caverns is a motorcyclists' dream; twisty, curvy, and lots of scenery, except for the 45 mph speed limit and constant patrol by park police. We ended up in a line of cars behind an RV. This is probably a good thing, as I would not have been able to resist tweaking "The Dragon" a bit. We slowly but steadily worked our way through the canyons and up the plateau, enjoying the scenery and cool air all the way. We parked amongst about 30 other motorcycles in the lot and paid our entrance fee.

There are two ways into the caves...you walk in the natural entrance on a steep but well-maintained trail, or you can ride down 700 feet in the elevators for an extra fee. Whichever way you go in, when you are done exploring the caves you come out the elevators. We elected to walk in, as you see much more of the caves that way. About 2-1/2 hours later we had made it through all the open trails.

Spectacular. Carlsbad is a must see. The scale of the cave system is amazing, and I am completely unable to describe it or photograph it in a way that really gets the size of it across. That was to be a common theme this trip.

We were amused by the rule that you could not carry anything to drink or eat...had no real conflict there, I wasn't there to eat, and any that have seen me know that I am in no danger of starving anytime soon, but it was on the premise that the smells would attract local wild-life to enter the cave and get lost. Okay...so why are they selling hot-dogs, hamburgers, and cokes at the concession stands at the very end of the trail, deep within the caves? (I have no problem with that either, I just wish they would play it straight once and a while).

There is postal drop box in the bottom of the cave that gets its own unique postmark, and I intended to mail cards from there...I bought the cards at the concession, but had left my addresses and stamps on the bike. No way I was walking back to get it. I would mail the cards later.

I set up the camera for a timer shot and managed to accidentally shoot James with the flash when he was not expecting it (that's my story and I am sticking to it). He looks pissed, but that was to be the norm. I have pictures of James looking pissed off in 4 different states and one of the pictures has him looking pissed in 4 states at the same time! He insists he was having a good time, but while he is an excellent photographer, just does not do well in front of the camera.

Let There Be Light!

We exited the caves into an intensely bright morning and headed for the bikes, blinking rapidly while our eyes adjusted from the deep dark-ness of the caves to the hot, bright, and barren landscape. We were slightly perplexed that all the motorcycles had vanished without a trace. Only our two were left in the lot. Something we said I guess...Grinned, shrugged, and mounted up. I had the slightly evil thought that they were probably traveling as a group, and I wondered if they thought they had lost a couple people in the caves due to the extra (our) bikes left in the lot when they pulled out.

We headed back through Carlsbad, and then up toward Roswell. The scenery out there is again a bit desolate, but due to the hour it was cool, and the riding was quite pleasant. Given how hot it gets in the afternoons, and how very pleasant it was during the morning, both James and I were surprised that folks were not up and about earlier. Except for the parking lot at the caves, the roadways were mostly deserted.

We wandered through Roswell looking for a decent photo-op but really found nothing exciting. Honestly we were looking for a real alien…we were going to whack him on the head and steal his space-ship. Perhaps they know this, as all the aliens managed to avoid us completely. Drat. The Visitors Bureau (for humans) was locked up tight. Apparently they do not expect any visitors on Sunday. After all, who travels on the weekends?

We stopped for lunch at an upscale-looking steak joint on the main drag. They either hate motorcyclists, or they are not very good at what they do. The service sucked, and we were attacked by another SCFS (Stealth Chicken Fried Steak). Blah. Got to watch those things. They can take you out. Once again, it was on top of the gravy. We have now learned that that is a bad sign. Thirty bucks for two lunch-CFS and soft drinks. No dessert. No wonder we could not find any aliens, the high prices, bad service, and terrible food chased them off.

We caught US 380 out of Roswell and headed west. This road is another good road for motorcycles. It winds around in some desert scenery—lots of twisties, then for kicks, drops down, crossing hot plains and going perfectly straight for miles. And miles. And miles.

I will state for the record, if headed west, get a tinted helmet visor. Mine was indispensable. Of course I had to carry a clear one also, but it is worth the trouble. Hours of driving into the sun will made me really appreciate it.

We arrived at Socorro at dusk. We had intended on getting into Arizona today, but we were not going to make it. Did not bother us a bit, we had entered "vacation time" now. We would get there when we got there. We grabbed a Hotel 6 again, cranked the AC down to "ball-shrinker", and went to find some dinner. A couple Smirnoff Ice went down nice and we hit the sack.

Zonk.

DAY THREE

Brrrrrrrrrrrr......

We awoke to temperatures in the 40's. Not outside, it never got below 80 at Socorro, but inside. We had finally found a hotel with an air conditioner that really works! Cool! Really!

We had an excellent and inexpensive breakfast at "Tina's Hideaway Café". Service was good, food was great, and prices were reasonable. Pancakes, sausage, eggs, ham, iced tea, and strawberries made for a great start to the day.

We caught US 60 west out of Socorro and climbed into the Datil Mountains. James began to experience trouble climbing the hills. The Honda GL 1100 was always known to be a bit underpowered for mountain climbing, but we have been up grades before without this much trouble. Something was wrong.

One of the luxuries about having radios is that we were able to continue on as best we could while discussing the problem. We could even experiment as we thought of things, as we were already moving. As we continued to climb and the temperature went up, the problem got worse.

We stopped to snap a couple pictures of "NRAOVLAT". No, we had not finally found our alien to ship-jack. "NRAOVLAT" is the "National Radio Astronomy Observatory Very Large Array Telescope". Phew! What a mouthful. I would have named it "BFA" for Big...ur...Array. Or maybe RBFA. Anyway this thing is a giant "X" on a high plateau covering several miles and consisting of unbelievably huge dish antennas. Quite a thing to see, and I'll bet they get all the cable channels.

Pulling out of there we decided we would not make Show-Low with James' bike mis-behaving. We had worked out a theory, and that was that "Bunnie" was starving for gas. The 1981 Gold Wing is not gravity feed fuel. The tank is positioned low in the frame, under the seat. What appears to be the tank is a plastic cover that houses some compartments, the fuel filler, and fuse and ignition boxes. Because of the tank position, the GoldWing has a fuel pump and must pump fuel uphill from the tank.

We were finding air in the fuel filter that is positioned between the petcock (fuel control valve) and the fuel pump. This means we are sucking air somewhere. We finally decided it was the petcock.

We stopped in Datil, pulling into the shade of an abandoned gas station with a sigh of relief. Shade is a valued commodity and in short supply out here.

We slobbered the petcock with some RTV sealant—an essential component of any travel kit—and walked across the road to the non-abandoned gas station to get a hamburger and a Diet Coke while we waited for the RTV to set. We were not worried about gluing the petcock into place; Since James' reserve does not function anyway. He never needs to turn the petcock.

We finished our burgers, moved the bikes across the street to gas them up, and took off. James' bike was performing fine. This was to be our only mechanical problem on the entire trip.

We pulled into Show-Low, decided that camping was in order. Unfortunately we were discovering that the National Forests were off limits to all but police and Forest Service employees due to fire danger. This was very carefully not mentioned on the Forest Service's website when we were planning this trip. This concerns me, as there is always the potential for fire, and some of these forests have been closed for two years. Are they taking this part of my heritage away from me too? It is also a bit annoying that two of the big fires were actually started by Forest Service employees or firefighters.

The advantage of camping in the national forests is that it is free to everyone. But now the current rules say you cannot venture there anymore, you must camp in developed (pay) camping sites. Of course they have eliminated most of those, making them day-use only areas. The rates for the "developed" sites are high, ten dollars for what amounts to a stake to hang your receipt on. No other facilities. Pretty sad. You are better off with a state park, National Recreation Area, or a KOA.

We pulled into Full-Hollow Lake Recreation Area. Pretty nice park, but a bit pricey. Also the lake is about the size of what we call a stock pond here in Texas.

Because it was a Monday, the ranger station was not staffed. The camping rate sign was a bit confusing. We only wanted one site, but the rate was listed for each vehicle. It also warned in impolite terms of dire consequences it you did not have a card in each vehicle. We could not decide if they wanted ten bucks or twenty. Was the envelope and thus the fee for a campsite, or a vehicle? Finally I simply gave up, tore a twenty-dollar bill in half and put half in each pay envelope. They could figure it out.

We set up camp, then went back to explore the town and pick up some drinks and munchies. Campfires were banned at the moment, so we spent a pleasant and cool evening sitting at our table talking and munching.

The cool air, the amazing vista of stars, and a day's worth of heat and riding soon blotted out the world.

Ummmm...That looks an awful lot like a Dragon...

Zonk.

DAY FOUR

Floating silently through the mist, almost without form, I am separated from my bike. I am unaware of feet, hands, ground, or sky. I am manifested as a fiery free spirit. Great wings, powerful muscles, passion infusing my soul. I imagine myself as a Pegasus, potent, intensely alive, always ready, flying and free. I can feel the power coursing through my veins, pulsing with my blood. The world is my domain, and I move freely within it. The destination is not relevant. Experience is life and passion is sustenance. The journey is the destination.

My bike is nicknamed "The Dragon", a name that she gave herself very early in our relationship, and today I know why. She is manifested as a huge dragon, flying along beside me, swift and silent, her black scales glistening with an almost translucent appearance, as if she were fashioned out of thousands of gemstones. Her wingspan would dwarf any dinosaur yet discovered, and her talons could rend a truck to nothing. Expressive and brilliant blue eyes peer at me and through me. She gives a playful flick of her tail to change direction and vanishes into the mist.

I know exactly where "The Dragon" is however. There is a spiritual connection between man, soul, machine, and road, and right now for some reason, to me it is visible, manifesting itself as a series of colored lines connecting us together and burning their way through the mist. Brilliant greens, vivid blues, and reds so bright they produce a corona run between us, small lightening bolts and other obvious energy traveling rapidly along the lines. The Dragon is ready, I am ready, and the road is always ready. All are calling to each other, and the lines are pulling us all inexorably together. Soon…again…we shall be one.

......<ping>

On day four we awoke to…*nothing.*
Pure, refined, distilled, 100-percent, crystal-clean…*nothing.*

The absolute silence only possible on a cool mountain morning greeted us with the promise of another gorgeous day. The cool night and mountain air had provided an extremely restful night's sleep, and the false dawn through the tent wall was my alarm clock. Shortly I could hear James stirring in the next tent also.

Few words were exchanged as we packed up the camp and loaded the bikes. Shortly we were on the road in the wonderful morning air.

We headed North on Arizona 77 toward Holbrook. We were going to spend a little time on the super-slab today (Interstate-40). We figured on breakfast when we needed to stop for gas. We caught Interstate-40 and headed west. We were planning on making the North Rim today, with a stop for Meteor Crater on the way.

Have you detected a theme for this trip yet? We had. Seemed to be a "hole in the ground" tour. Cool, as the destination is just the excuse, but it at least ought to be interesting.

Arizona's finest were out fleecing the tourists, so we pegged the speed at 75–80, set the cruise, and left it. We spotted 12 cruisers within about 30 miles; a rough calculation and we figure they are bringing in about $8000 per hour. This is more officers than we saw the entire rest of the trip. If crime is so low in Arizona that you can put 20 guys on a 30-mile stretch of road, then here is a hint, fire the cops and put a couple more cents tax on the gas. I'll take my chances with the speeders, rather than with the cop cars and tourists parked all over the Interstate, not to mention the police cruisers turning around in the median and scattering dust, gravel, and unwary travelers that happen to be in their path.

We pulled off at Winslow to fuel up the bikes and ourselves. You gotta love someone that would chrome an entire Denny's restaurant. We ate about half a pig (bacon, ham, and sausage) as well as eggs and pancakes. Diet Coke and Iced Tea for drinks. When the waitress asked if we needed anything else, James looked up and ordered—of all things—a hot-fudge ice-cream sundae!

A hot-fudge sundae for dessert, at breakfast! *Hrumph*.

I looked James in the eye and calmly said, "You're going to Hell for that you know..."

Then, of course, I ordered one for myself. James said, "And you're coming with me."

The waitress was still waiting so I nodded at her and said, "Apparently we are both going to Hell."

The waitress did not even blink.

And I was right...although we did not know it yet.

We got back onto the super-slab for a few miles, then followed the signs to Meteor Crater.

The coming heat was beginning to announce itself as we climbed up to the top observation platform. Several folks traded cameras for the obligatory picture, and when the guy that took our picture handed the digital camera back to me he gave me an odd look. I was unsure why until we saw the picture that night as we unloaded the images. Apparently he had seen it "saving" in the viewfinder and could not quite bring himself to say anything. You see, James looks like he is shoving his finger down his throat...kind of an editorial comment or something. James swears that he was pushing his glasses up...sounds like a good story. Yeah.

We both liked the crater; although at twelve dollars it is a bit expensive to see and you cannot go into the crater, just view it from the edge. Imagining the impact that produced this conflagration is somewhat sobering.

We also liked it because it was not a state park, national monument, or public land. It is privately held. Kind of neat, and unusual. Good conversation starter too..."Yeah, I own a crater in the middle of the Arizona Desert, what do you do?"

Into Hell

We hit the road again, and shortly we were cruising up US 89 toward the North Rim. This is all Navajo Indian reservation, and the further North we went, the hotter and more desolate it became. The temperatures were in the triple digits and continually climbing, and the sun was relentless. As we topped each rise, and a valley revealed itself to be even more desolate then the previous one, we kept expecting it to be the last. Finally in one area there was no vegetation at all, and even the dirt looked burned. It very much resembled the tailings of a strip mine, but this was not man-made.

I felt a great respect for those that came this way before there was an asphalt ribbon to travel at high-speed upon. When topping a rise and finding miles more of hostile land in front of them, how and why did they carry on? I felt awe at the Navajos' ability to survive here. I also felt some pity for the Christian Missionaries that hoped to teach the confined Navajos about the Christian faith. I can only imagine that if they managed to get their concept of Heaven and Hell across to the Indians, that the Indians could only look around and say, "Hell, huh? So...?"

Somewhere in the middle of all this James keyed up the radio and said, "You're right. We are here."

Hell, huh…?

This is the kind of area that requires as much water to drink as gas for the bike, so we were stopping frequently for breaks. I am a Texan, and am used to the heat, but combined with the extremely low humidity here, incredible amounts of water are lost through sweat and simply breathing. In an attempt to remain hydrated, we started drinking before we entered this area and continued long afterward. Water can be lost faster then it can be absorbed, but care is required as it is also possible to overdo it and drink too much, causing injury and even death (do a little research on "water toxicity"). Occasional soda's (high sodium content), salt tablets, salty snacks, or sports drinks are necessary. There is a balance to achieve, and the body will make that clear, once the signs are understood.

I found a strange kind of peace in the desolation and the heat and barren landscape. I had much time to reflect, and there is nothing quite like exposing ourselves to nature to understand our place in it. I and my machine were sorely tested, and I will be back this way again.

The ride on Alt 89 to Jacob Lake was incredible. The Vermillion Cliffs are another must-see. My favorite picture of the entire trip...the one that sums up the entire reason for a trip like this, was taken here. In 90 miles the road passes through desert and the Vermillion Cliffs, then climbs out of the desert and several thousand feet up to the plateau. Suddenly it is winding through cool, luxurious forest. What a road!

We reached Jacob Lake and stopped for gas and lunch. This is a logical staging area for seeing the North Rim, as it is nearly 100 miles round-trip down the park road to reach the rim. They close at 7pm, but their pumps are open 24/7 for credit cards. Handy for motorcycles; there is not much fuel out here. They were reasonable on the price, but the burgers reminded me much of my high-school cafeteria. Not bad, just not remarkable.

We got quite a laugh when James asked if they made hot-fudge sundaes.

The waitress bubbled over with enthusiasm, "Sure we do!"

Then, "Well, not really. We don't have hot-fudge." Then she brightened up again, "We do have some chocolate-like stuff though...we could heat it up for you!" We declined.

Friendly folks though. Stop and see 'em.

Into the park we went. The road is worth the trip, even if there had not been a gorgeous canyon at the end of it. Twisties, forest, valleys, cool temperatures, and the stunning sky made riding this road worth the entire trip. I'll be back.

The Grand Canyon is...well...Grand. Again, I am completely unable to describe it in a way that will get the scale of it across. Here is how you can do it. Get on your bike and drive there. Really.

The required picture again, we traded cameras with a big Harley-biker looking dude...he was out on the observation platform and his wife was trying to get a picture. He was insisting that she hurry as the

Canyon at his back was freaking him out. It really is that impressive. After she got the picture, he rapidly started to get away from the edge. Of course I, with my slightly evil disposition, asked his wife if she would like me to take a picture of them both together on the edge, he was behind her frantically nodding "no", but she said, "Oh that would be great!" and he had to step back out there again. I relented though, and rapidly took their picture. He was much relived to get away from the edge. There was a substantial railing on the platform, but I guess everyone is afraid of something.

Of course James's picture is odd…but that is tradition by now.

We stopped for gas again at Jacob Lake on the way out. I had been sending postcards each day to my wife and some family and friends. The ones I penned here said simply "Yahoooooo!" scrawled across the back, with the Grand Canyon on the front. They would all get the message.

We spent more time on that wonderful road on the way back out, and made our way over 100 miles to the town of Page to grab some dinner and a hotel.

We explored the town a bit, picked up some Chap-Stick (forgotten and by now sorely needed), set the AC for "Ice Age", and hit the hay.

I briefly pondered the trip so far, then suddenly and vividly re-entered my dream of the night before.

Soaring, flying, free…

Zonk.

DAY FIVE

We slept in a bit on day five. The heat and miles were finally taking some of their toll, and a couple hours extra sleep was just the thing. After all, we were on vacation time anyway.

Page is a cool town. It is situated on a hillside overlooking the dam for Lake Powell. A very impressive view. The main street is a "U" going up the hill from US 89 through the town and then back down the hill to US 89 again. A somewhat odd and possibly unique arrangement. Looked like an interesting place.

We pulled out of Page on Arizona 98, headed for a connection to US 160. We were hitting 4-Corners today, then on into Durango. Arizona 98 was hot and desolate, but has one outstanding trait that no other road on our entire trip possessed—it had no construction on it whatsoever. On every other road, we encountered at least one area of construction.

Arizona 98 is also where we found the valley of the dust-devils. We topped a hill and an incredible vista was presented, a massive valley, with virtually no vegetation, but seemingly teaming with life. There were hundreds of dust-devils wandering all over the valley. From tiny ones only a couple feet tall, to mammoth beasties the size of a sky-scraper, they were all there. We could witness them coming to life, dancing around in ecstasy, and then occasionally dying, their life force scattering and contributing to the birth of others.

As we headed down into the valley I idly wondered what it would be like to ride through one of them. I was soon to get my question answered, as an extremely large one was approaching the road as we reached the bottom of the hill.

They lost visual definition as we approached them, the closer we got the less we could see them. I lost sight of the large one, but it did not lose sight of us…*bang*, whoosh, it attacked. What an amazing, if short-lived force. It was at least 20 degrees cooler in the core, and felt very strange, almost electric. James commented that it nearly twisted his helmet off.

I could not help but wonder if we caused it any injury…

Four-Corners is kind of odd. Basically, somebody placed a dot on a map, said firmly that the dot is *here*, and planted a rock. It is a monument to two imaginary lines intersecting. Some Indians then set up souvenir stands to make a few bucks from the nutcases that drive all the way out into the desert to see it (umm…that would be us…).

I bought the obligatory present for the wife, and took the pictures required. Now I have one of James looking pissed off in 4 different states at the same time. He still insists he was having a good time.

There were a couple other motorcyclists there, and I found myself staring at one guy. He was staring back. It seemed I knew him, but I could not figure out from where. So of course we struck up a conversation.

Turned out he had been at Meteor Crater, and the North Rim at the same time we were, and at Carlsbad the same day we were. Now we had met at Four-Corners, and he was heading for Durango. It is a great big world, but still small in surprising ways. I meet the most interesting people in the most interesting places on motorcycles.

Between Cortez and Durango we encountered a bunch of crazy people. Hundreds of people on bicycles were riding in some kind of event, and were strung out along the road for many miles. It takes some guts, strength, and a little bit of strangeness to ride a bicycle up the mountain passes, and we were to pass these folks for the next two days! Amazing!

We had been in the smoke from the Colorado and New Mexico fires for days, but Durango was the central point for fighting one of the large ones. Visibility in the mountains was down to ¼ mile at times, and Durango was overrun with firefighters, as well as bicyclists from the event, *and* a charity motorcycle run. Most hotels were sold out, and all the surrounding forests were closed. There was some mighty interesting equipment arriving on trucks for the firefighters. We were beginning to wonder if we were going to have to sleep in a parking lot, but finally located a room at a lodge at the edge of town.

I liked the attitude of lady that was running the place. I took the room (there were no more) and then asked if it was a smoking room.

She warily looked at me and asked, "Do you want to smoke in the room?"

I said, "Yep." (James smokes cigars).

She then handed me an ashtray and said, "Then it is a smoking room."

Kind of refreshing, after all the militant non-smoking nuts running about. Even if I did smoke, I would not have needed to in Colorado. The smoke from the fires was plenty.

We unloaded the bikes, then explored the town a bit. Grabbed some dinner, then a 6-pack of Smirnoff Ice and headed back to the lodge.

We spent some time talking about the trip so far, turned the AC to…oh wait…there was no AC, it is not needed in Durango, and later hit the sack.

I found myself reflecting that we were basically headed east now…more or less heading home. I penned a postcard to my wife;

The distance between us,
is measured just in miles.
Our souls are still connected,
but I really miss your smile.
Soon we'll be together,
'cause though I need to roam.
My wanderlust is sated,
"The Dragon's" headed home.

I ponder the trip some more, then I gratefully reentered the running dream from the last few nights.

I spread my wings, cry out in ecstasy, and fly.

Zonk.

Day Six

Soaring, the Dragon and I, effortlessly viewing the lands below us. Hungry for more experience, we twist to the left and change direction. Whole new vistas appear before us. Again a twist, and another new world appears. A twist back to the original path does not reveal the original world—it is subtly changed. The world is a mystical and magical place, and is always in motion. Those that view the world as a static or boring place simply do not know how to look, how to really see. I can see—I know how. I know deep in my soul that I could experience this forever without tiring of it, and the Dragon promptly roars in agreement at that thought. Another twist, and off we go to explore another world.

......<ping>...

The morning of Day 6 treated us to our first real jacket weather on the trip. Temperatures were in the 40's, and the smoke had settled over the town like a seaport fog. We loaded the bikes and had a leisurely breakfast. As is our custom, the bikes had been gassed up the night before. We have never had a problem, but it seems prudent to be ready to leave a strange area at a moment's notice, particularly if the area is surrounded by fires.

We saw lots of construction on the trip, but usually I do not comment too heavily about the nature of it. I love our highway system, and it needs continual maintenance and upgrading. If they are making any attempt to keep the delays to the minimum then I really do not sweat it.

However I really must comment on a dangerous bit of construction that was going on where US 160 entered Durango. I have no idea why, but they were cutting lots of lines into the concrete road in a cross pattern (expansion/break joints?). It looked like they had been doing this all over the road for days. This can be (is) highly dangerous to motorcyclists. The saw that they use to cut the concrete requires water lubrication, and the water carries the concrete dust as it runs off. This produces an *extremely* slippery slurry on the road. It is quite frankly more slippery than a puddle of motor-oil, indeed approaching being as slippery as a patch of ice. As long as it is wet, it is a hazard. Today, they were cutting around an intersection, and the slurry was running through several of the turn lanes. There were a lot of motorcycles in town; I hope we did not lose any. Beware.

We headed for Ouray on US 550. This is a fun road for motorcycles. There are two passes between Durango and Ouray that are over 10,000 feet. We had a blast, even though the smoke was obscuring some of the scenery. Once again, we were passing bicyclists that were climbing the passes. Hundreds of them. These are some tough folks, peddling up a 10,000 foot pass is not for the faint of heart. We paced a guy for a moment going down the other side. I did not know you could get a bicycle to 55 mph, even down hill! I wonder if the pleasure of going down the hill is worth the pain of going up the hill.

I had been looking forward to Ouray. The wife and I had visited several years before and found it to be a pleasant and friendly place. The hot spring pools were worth visiting, and I felt that a soak would do me some good.

Unfortunately, Ouray has been discovered. It was overrun with tourists. Obnoxious ones, ones that like to park in the middle of the street, and apparently do not worry about running over motorcyclists. You could not have squeezed into the hot springs sideways, and if any additional vehicles parked on the main drag the town would reach critical mass and turn into a black hole. We gassed up and moved on.

We grabbed some grub in Montrose (another Chromed Denny's) and headed for...another hole in the ground. Black Canyon of the Gunnison is worth the trip. It is a National Monument, and had a rather odd sign on the road. "Unload guns and secure all ammunition". *What?* I had visions of dozens of cars pulled off to the side of the road to comply. Get real guys.

After viewing the canyon, we spent the next several hours trying to find a campsite. Unfortunately again, the National Forest was closed, apparently to allow Forest Service Employees privacy to start their own deliberate fires. Pretty sad.

All but two of the developed campsites in this area (dozens) have been converted to "day use only", and of the two remaining; one of them only had 2 sites and no facilities. For this they want 10 bucks. I am seriously concerned, as the trend seems to be to prohibit and discourage the public from actually making use of the lands that are a significant portion of their heritage. I will be watching this...

We were still passing bicyclists. I upped my estimate of their numbers from hundreds to thousands. I must admit, James (and my CB) saved my life on this stretch of road. I was leading, and we were in some twisties and pushing hard, going uphill, when we passed a lone bicyclist. Suffice it to say, one must be in very good shape to attempt this ride, and this cyclist was in *very* good shape. *She* was also wearing tight, tiger-striped spandex, and as she was going uphill, she was standing and bent way over on her bike peddling furiously. This causes wiggles and shapes that inevitably and firmly attract and hold the attention of a male.

Hmmmm...yummi.

Suddenly the radio crackled, "Watch the road, not the broad!" I quickly but reluctantly forced my attention elsewhere and managed to barely avoid driving off a cliff.

What can I say? I am a guy after all...

We grabbed a KOA in Gunnison (very clean park and friendly folks) and set up camp. We had a late lunch so we skipped dinner although we could have ordered pizza delivered to our tent if we wanted! (How about that?) We did some laundry, and passed the time the machines were running playing some pool.

As I lay in my tent listening to the thunder (it never did rain) I wondered if I was really ready to go home.

Once again, the Dragon called. There were many more twists yet unexplored…

Zonk.

DAY SEVEN

The Dragon flying beside me is magnificent, but somehow out of place. She seems to be missing something, lacking completeness. I ponder the joy and experience of the past few days and realize that despite all the fun, I am missing something too. There is a hole in a piece of me that cries for fulfillment.

Suddenly I notice that the vivid colored lines connecting us together are getting even brighter, somehow thicker, and their pull is very powerful. For some days, the man, the Dragon, the soul, and the road were slowly being drawn together. Finally and belatedly we realize that we are together, and always have been, even though sometimes we have forgotten. Apart we are unable to function, unable to dream, and unable to truly exist.

At that moment lightening travels rapidly along the colored lines, and we are swiftly drawn together. Rather than avoiding a collision, we embrace it. Man and Dragon merge into an intense ball of light, cry out in ecstasy, and suddenly we are one. Finally we know. Finally we see. None can exist without the others. We cannot survive separately, and the road, passion, and experience are the food for our soul. We must continue to pursue them all.

Man, Dragon, soul, and road all rejoice.

......<ping>...

I again awoke extremely refreshed. I lay there enjoying the coolness, it seemed I was still shedding the heat from the past few days. Thinking about my dreams, I finally understood the message. I guess I had really known it all along, but the pressures of life often try to make me forget. They will not succeed again.

I listened to the gentle burbling of the creek right behind my tent, gave a deep sigh, and began to break camp.

More Bicyclists:

We sucked up another huge breakfast (hot-fudge sundaes and all) and hit the road. Today's destination was Clayton Lake State Park in New Mexico or perhaps as far as Amarillo, Texas. We headed east on US 50 toward Pueblo and I-25. We would then head south and split off on US 87 at Raton.

US 50 is another fun road, and again we were passing bicyclists climbing the passes. How far were these guys going? They were spread out over about 80 miles of road, which is very impressive. I am glad my cycle has an engine!

As we were on motors, we had the power and room to get around the bicyclists, cages, and motor homes that were all caught in an ugly mix. We had a really good time in the twisties, and the weather could not have been better.

That is, until we reached Pueblo and the super-slab.

From the moment we got on I-25 we were ruthlessly pounded by vicious crosswinds, gusting as high as 50 mph. This can be very wearing, and we were in them from Pueblo to well past Raton, a distance of over 150 miles. This is extremely tiring, and can make riding a real chore, no matter how much we normally enjoy it. Results of this kind of riding can range from sore muscles to actual bruises and chafed skin if clothing is loose or flapping.

As we neared the Texas border, the sun went down, and the winds died with it. Suddenly riding was sheer ecstasy, and we could not have ordered up better conditions for it. As much fun as we had experienced so far, we had not had riding conditions that were so perfect. We decided it must be some sort of sin to stop under these circumstances, and we would keep going and only stop when we got tired.

About 500 miles later we were home (860 for the day). Drat. I was not really ready.

We went "Hell and Gone" seeking something. I think we found it.

I learned several things:

- Dust Devils are alive.

- Colorado is beautiful, even when it is on fire.

- New Mexico and Arizona are rugged, hot, arid, and desolate. And I love them both.

- The postal service picked a really bad time to raise their rates. I beat all but 2 of my postcards home. I had been mailing them since the first day out. *Not* impressive.

- This is a bloody big country. The best way to see this, is to get out in it, preferably on a motorcycle. Urban sprawl is a myth. 90% of the population is on 5% of the land.

- I am not a Valkyrie rider, I am a Valkyrie Pilot. That speedometer goes to 145mph for a reason. *Wow.*

- I will never again allow the pressures of life to disconnect me from my *self.* I will not give up the experiences and people I love so that I somehow fit a social norm or societal role. To do so is the death of the soul.

- My friends are my most valuable resource.

- To paraphrase Shakespeare, I learned that, 'There are more things in heaven and earth, than are dreamt of in our philosophy.'

- Small Texas towns are interesting on Friday night. There is still "cruising" going on, folks out on the main drag showing off cars, meeting each other, and talking. They will start up a conversation even with a 300-pound biker dude from out of town. By contrast, Dallas is dead. If not paying $$ in a club, the social scene is just not there. There are places in Dallas where tickets are handed out for driving up the same road twice in one night (to prevent cruising). The small towns are much better, I can actually meet people. I am going to explore this further.

- As big as this country is, I ran out of road way too soon. Next time I will have to go out further before I turn around. I am already planning…

But I knew all that already, so what did I really find? What were we seeking, what did we find? What was *it*?

Well, sorry. I cannot tell you, I can only show you. *It* is palely reflected in these writings somewhere, and I hope I was able to help you find your own way to see it. If you did not find it here, or even if you did, go—get on your bike and ride.

It…is out *there*.

Into the Maelstrom

Dallas got clobbered in the wee night hours of August 27 (surprise!) by a massive wall of violent and unpredicted thunderstorms. Internal winds reached 70 mph, and the outflow boundaries exceeded that. Some property damage was done, and hundreds of thousands were without power well into the next day.

The line pounced on us from the northwest, moving at over 50 mph.

Not sure if what follows meets the technical definition for a poem, or what…but it is what came out…

Into the Maelstrom

Swiftly I ride.
Frequently looking back into the night.
There is beauty, and splendor, and terrifying power behind.
I am hunted, and this kind has hunted me before.

But I am The Dragon.
A complicated, intimate union between passionate man and
    intricate machine.
And power I possess in my own right.
I laugh and twist the throttle more.

But this hunter is swift and decisive.
Very big and brutishly violent.
Following, gaining, sure and focused.
Relentlessly it stalks me.

I can fly, but not in the fashion of my pursuer.
So my route is indirect.
I can hear him now, feel his breath.
My hunter gains.

Closer he comes, so sure of his catch.
I can see others fleeing his path.
Some trying to warn me of what is behind.
Another turn and I am sure, we will meet.

A conflict now is imminent.
I sigh and prepare myself.
And I smile, a dangerous smile.
My reaction is not the one expected.

He pounces, primal violence unleashed.
Rarely have I felt the like.
And I have been hunted by many of his kind.
Lightning bolts fly.

I scream defiance into the storm.
The Dragon plows on, our course unaltered.
I laugh out loud in sheer joy, or maybe madness.
The storm howls in frustration and redoubles his efforts.

Others huddle in the shelter of a bridge, while works of man
    and nature fall.
The Dragon and I fly by.
Whooping, laughing, reveling.
Maybe crying.

Its force spent quickly by its very violence, the storm finally
   fades.

On the air a promise to return, to finish the hunt.

Then something else on the air, a fleeting thought, a pang of
   fear.

Is the prey...really the prey?

My mind is clear, my tension released.

My life is mine.

And I like that it is in my hands.

As I am the only one qualified to guard it.

Speeding ever onward, roaring into the night.

I think of those huddled.

The difference between us is clear.

They are victims, reacting to attack.

I am a participant, reveling in the experience.

Never passive, never fearing, always seeking.

To the storm my message is clear.

Although not very eloquent:

"Is that all you've got? HA! You'll have to do better than
   that!"

Is the prey...really the prey?

Her, The Dragon, and Me

How can you not believe in magic?
Having lived very long in this world.
Traveled the roads.
Seen the sheer scope.
Screamed defiance into the storms.

Magic is everywhere.
Can you not see?
It is most easily found in the arms of a woman.
Those beautiful creatures that hold our souls in their hands.
We are un-tempered without their union.

But there is a danger.
They can crush the soul.
They can kill the man within.
Or they can lift him to heights unimagined.
Those whose peers have caused them to believe they have no
    power.

No power indeed.

What power, ask you?
Only the power of creation.
Only the power of life.

Just that would be enough.
But there is even more.

One such creature holds my destiny.
Magic. She is magic, defined and uncontained.
Quieting my soul.
Stirring my dreams.
Taking the pain away.

Filling the gaps.
Plugging the holes.
Moderating the strength.
Making life bearable.
Showing me the magic.

Yet she does not truly know me.
Even after all this time.
Does not really understand.
The dark-side of the man.
The torment in my soul.

The yearnings of my heart.
The strength.
The lust.
The urge.
The power.

The requirements of my soul.
The open road, The Dragon and me.
Riding into the storm.

The overwhelming lust for life.
This devastating need to *see*.

For her, what do I feel?
It is way too sexual for just love.
It is a little too quiet for simple lust.
It is magic.
There is no other word.

The storm and the woman.
The are the same, and they are magic.
They can bring life to the world.
Or death to the soul.
Equally beautiful, equally terrifying, in either role.

My destiny is open.
My life is free.
But still She has the power.
What will we make of it?
Her, The Dragon, and me?

The Dragon is Calling

I went for a really long ride yesterday. I am not really sure I understand this need, this compulsion to voyage…as I once phrased it… *"This devastating need to see…"*

Even if I should come to understand it, I have no intention of excising it. That would be kin to cutting out a healthy portion of my soul.

I commute on my bike daily, but I really yearn for the open roads. I have been known to make trips several thousand miles long, and take at least one long trip yearly.

There is something very primal in riding—a solid, tangible connection between man, road, and machine. Definitely spiritual, probably a bit sexual, maybe wrapped up in the very forces of life itself. Then again, maybe it is just me. When riding, I am having fun, but that is not why I am there. When I am riding, more so than at any other time, well, I just *am*. With time away from the road, those connections do not weaken, they become stronger, pull harder. They are eventually impossible to resist.

I had worked on the boat in the morning. Eventually, as happens in the Texas summer, the heat forced me to quit.

Headed home and cleaned up. The evening was shaping up to be a nice one, as the promised cool front was hanging around overhead, finally bringing a little cooler and drier air.

Said, "Heck with it" and hopped on "The Dragon". Man! I love to ride that beast. And she is really built for it…huge, 775 pounds dry, well over half a ton with me and fuel, and the longest wheelbase of any cruiser other than the Gold Wing. Yet she is amazingly nimble and maneuverable, out classing many. The power and torque throughout her entire gear and rpm range are nothing short of amazing. When I twist the throttle on this monster, I really have to hang on. My size and strength are a complement to her, and together we are a single being. I *become* "The Dragon".

Of course I may be just a bit biased.

I headed north out of Dallas, hit Sherman 70 miles or so later, then headed back south on TX 5, intending to head for home. Nearly at McKinney, I changed my mind and headed northeast on US121 and ran to Bonham. I wandered around town a bit, looking closely at a 130+ year-old house that my mother once owned (restoration project).

Then it was east to Paris. Stopped at a KFC, ate some chicken, and flirted with the cute KFC gal. Yum. The chicken was ok too. Stopped to take a picture of a dragon (not mine, and not a motorcycle). Nice town, but oddly laid out.

Left town and headed south for Commerce, where while stopped at a convenience store for a Coke, I got a new gun. Commerce is a college town, and as such, has more than its fair share of drunk college kids.

One of those made three BIG mistakes.

Mistake #1—Pulling a gun on a Texan, especially one who is minding his own business. I think they just thought they were going to give a little scare to the biker type dude (me).

Mistake #2—Not immediately firing it after pulling a gun on a Texan.

Mistake #3—See mistake # 1.

Our conversation was something like this:

Him, "Ahhhhhhhh."

Me, "Nice gun…thanks! You should have those broken fingers looked at pretty soon, or you will lose the use of your hand. And I think your nose is probably broken. Sorry about the busted windshield, if you had rolled when you landed, it probably would have held up ok."

Him, "AhhhhhhhOwwwwwwwwww."

He then barfed all over his car. Went well with the blood from his nose.

His friend was apologetic and promised to get him home and keep him out of trouble.

The gun was a cheap knockoff of Colt's famous 45 1911 auto…it had not been cleaned or fired recently. Yuck. As a Texan I should be offended that he did not pull a better gun on me. I know from personal experience that this particular brand is a complete junker. No accuracy, and no power to speak of, despite the hot load he had in it. I have given better guns away. Besides, I have enough 45 autos (good ones). I took it apart, and scattered pieces along the rest of my journey.

Drunks, cars, and guns. Sheesh, what a mix. Morons.

I think his car keys are in Lake Ray Hubbard.

The moral of that is twofold: 1) If you are going to draw on a Texan, you damn well better shoot, and 2) If you are looking for trouble, and you see a 6 foot, 300-pound biker type dude standing there minding his own business—you probably ought to pick someone else.

I avoided another drunk in a red pickup on US635 in Dallas, he seemed determined to run *someone* off the road.

Total of about 350 miles. Overall a really good evening. I am still smiling.

Of course, right now…I can hear "The Dragon" calling…

TeXSive Ride

The "TeXSive Ride" is an annual event for folks that ride or have owned Yamaha XS-1100 motorcycles. Although I now ride a Valkyrie, I have known and corresponded with several of these folks (XS'ives) in the past. Such is the camaraderie of motorcyclists, that I (and indeed anyone else that is interested) am welcome to attend. Riding...the journey...and the people met and things learned on the journey—is the point.

Poor Wayne. I distinctly remember he just mentioned that we should have a Texas ride-in.

Tag! You're it! Thanks for volunteering!

He also mentioned Kerrville. I believe I responded with something like, "<grunt, snort> Yah! Kerrville das good!" or something equally articulate.

Oh, by the way...he also said the word "annual" in there somewhere...again, thanks for volunteering! Keep me posted as to when and where the next one is...

So, here we go.

Even a hurricane could not stop it. Forecasts on September 23 put Hurricane Isador's center arriving exactly on Kerrville Friday the 27th, about the time that I was hoping to arrive at the campsite.

Nope, wouldn't do at all. Texas is a big state, but I am a big guy, and Isador is a big storm. There would not be room here for both of us. Pity Kerrville if we both arrived there at the same time. I committed to myself to go regardless of the weather...I needed the ride, I needed the experience. Oh, and Texans never bluff...not at anything important anyway.

There is a strange kind of life taken on by a powerful storm, an odd communication between the hunter and the prey…I have fought and been hunted by them before, on motorcycles, in planes, in boats, and on foot. I have always won. So many times now that the line between which is the hunter and which is the prey has begun to blur (*see Into the Maelstrom*).

Arrogant? Well, perhaps. Life is here to be experienced, experience is our purpose, and it will be all we take with us in the end. I am not stupid about it, but you cannot experience life, if you are avoiding all the experiences at the slightest excuses.

Whatever the reasons, Isador turned tail and went to cause problems in other states (sorry about that, but we had motorcycle riding to do!). By Wednesday it was apparent that the weather was no longer a factor. In fact, we could not have ordered better weather for this event had we been able to!

Friday morning I slept in a bit (normally I have to get up around 4:00am for work), finished loading "The Dragon", took my wife out for a leisurely breakfast, and much to the amusement of the restaurant patrons there, passionately kissed her goodbye. We got sporadic applause. I pulled out of Dallas around 9:00am.

Once again I chose my route with avoiding the super-slabs in mind. Due to constant construction, massive truck traffic, bleak scenery, and dazed cage drivers, Interstate-35 is boring and marginally unsafe for motorcycles.

I caught US67 out of Dallas, headed for US281 at Hico. US67 is a pain, it has been under construction for years, and they are apparently not getting anywhere. When I stopped for gas at Glen Rose, I nearly dumped "The Dragon", as they have constructed concrete curbs and edgings along the street, but paved the street with blacktop…which is for some reason about 3" below the level of the concrete edgings. I did not see the edge till I hit it in a mild turn into the parking lot. Guess I should have been watching closer, even though it is a brand new street.

Had to gas it and make a very aggressive turn to keep from dropping the big cruiser. Me and "The Dragon" understand each other.

The credit card slot on the pump was not working, so I selected "pay inside" and fueled her up. I needed some caffeine anyway. I pulled the Valkyrie off the pumps into the shade at the front of the store. As I entered the store, I caught the tail end of a tirade from some dirty-looking skinny guy. As he was leaving the store he was screaming, "I just want to get to Dallas, and a little gas would help! Dumb bitch!" He was trying to get it for free. As he exited the store, he intentionally ran into me, shoulder to shoulder.

Now I am normally polite, but I do not yield to or tolerate uncivil behavior. I saw him coming and as a result, he nearly went down when I did not budge, give, or sway. One advantage of being a fat guy, is that people continually underestimate your strength. For some reason they associate "fat" and "weak". Maybe true for some guys. Big mistake in my case. He looked startled, started to say something, thought better of it, and left the store. I made a point of watching him, keeping eye contact when he looked my way, until he got into his car and drove away.

The clerk was obviously upset and was holding back tears. As I approached the counter with my Diet Coke, she snapped at me, "And where are you trying to get to!"

I took no offense, she was upset and could be excused this. There was no one else in the store to snap at. I flashed my blue eyes at her and calmly said, "My business is mine, but at least I will pay for my gas…and my coke. You ok?"

At this she came back to the present, wiped a tear from her eye and began to apologize.

I held up my hand, "Not necessary. Some people are just jerks, or cons. Don't let them get to you."

"Why are you so nice?" she stammered as she continued to compose herself.

"Because I like people. Life would be a bore if we were all the same."

We finished the transaction, and I left the store. I stood outside next to my bike in the shade and sipped my coke, while stretching my legs. One reason I like "The Dragon" is that the massive gleaming cruiser always attracts comment, from riders and non-riders alike. I meet more interesting people touring, usually while standing in the shade and drinking my coke.

Shortly the clerk came out to join me. There were no other customers.

She was much more composed. She was in her 20's, with long brown hair tied in a single ponytail. About five feet tall or so. Long legs. Not supermodel material, but cute nonetheless. Basically, a green-eyed Texas girl. We do grow 'em nice here.

I usually have a sense about people. I liked her. She will go places.

"I'm Lisa."

I pointed at her nametag, "Then how come your nametag says 'Bob'?"

I was lying, but it got a laugh and she smiled. I then introduced myself.

A bit shyly she asked, "So…where are you going?"

"Kerrville."

"I don't know where that is. But can I come? I want out of here."

My people sense told me several things;

1) She was serious.

2) "Out of here" meant far more than away from the store.

3) The offer was comprehensive…she was offering herself and well…*herself* in exchange for a different life. Any different life.

4) She had never done this before.

5) I could also tell that she had been propositioned enough that she had a "view" of men, and she did not expect to be refused.

People are all different. For some, this may be ok…a new adventure. For her it was giving up on some dream. This was a kind of surrender for her.

Tempted? Well yes. I am a male after all. The desire is there. You cannot help but be flattered and tempted by such an offer. There are none that would not be. But more than a male, I am a *man*. Some…many…no longer know or care what that means. But I still do.

I know what is right. Always. But I do not always know how to do it or say it. After all, I am just a man.

"Sorry, no."

What followed was a rapid-fire explicit expansion of the offer and what it meant, sprinkled with a severe dose of self-doubt…the "I'm not pretty enough" type of stuff. Her view of men did not allow for refusal unless something was wrong with her.

I took her hand. "I understand…I get it…" That brought her to a stop. She was crying again. I hate it when that happens.

"You are very pretty. Were my situation different, I would want to know you better. But not like this. You are intelligent, pretty, healthy, and young, and you will get out of here…but there are better, other ways to do that, and if you think about it, you probably already know what they are. There are great things in your future. I'll bet you even have plans…?"

Hesitantly, "Yes." Then more firmly, "Yes." She looked up at me, meeting my eyes, suddenly comprehending something big. I think her worldview shifted. *Zap.* Just like that.

And then her eyes came alive, *"Yes."*

About this time a car pulled up to the pumps. She sniffed, smiled, and went into the store. She has some things to think about.

She will be all right. A juxtaposition had been reached, a little more about the world learned, and a course chosen.

Back on the road again. As I pulled away I reflected on what a difference a little thought or consideration could make.

All she needed was somebody who cared.

Strangely, I am elated. The world is…well…*connected*…soul, road, man, and machine. I know it, it was reaffirmed again, and I think I showed someone else that today. The world is magic. You get from it what you are looking for.

Finally out of the construction. As the speeds climbed, and the gorgeous weather and the music on my mp3 player further elated my mood, I realized I had things to think about too.

People are infinitely interesting and varied. It is too bad we are often short-sighted enough to experience pain and doubt when it is not truly necessary. Some feel this is essential to the "growing up" process, but I disagree. I decided that I still like my approach…participate, get out into the world, but always look for the interesting and for the magical. It is there for the taking, and there is plenty for everyone. The rest is all but inconsequential and will sort itself out.

This attitude, my ability and desire to look at the world with wide-eyed wonder, is often mistaken for naiveté by those that do not know me and the things I have been through. I can only look at them with a just bit of pity.

A stop in Lampasas for some fuel, and some lunch. Had a very mediocre chicken-fried steak at a cafeteria-style place. I feel sorry for the town if it is really "the best place in town" as I was told by the gas station lady. I usually ask where the best places for food are…usually I come out ahead and find a good place. Not this time. Oh well. What does not kill you makes you stronger, yes?

Except in Dallas, and in the construction on US 67, the roads had been deserted. The music and the weather, and the deserted roadways made for some intoxicating riding. Just how wrapped up in the riding I was became apparent when I was roaring down the road south of Lampasas, and eventually I passed a sign that said "Austin 22". Went on a bit before that finally registered. *Err…what?* Twenty-two miles to Austin? But…I was not going to Austin…well…at least I was not intending on going to Austin. *What the heck?*

Apparently I was not sure where I was going, but I sure was making good time! Holistic navigation—Essentially, you may not get where you intended to, but you *will* get somewhere you needed to be. I am famous for it.

Kept going until I found a sign that told me I was on US 183. Oops. Apparently there is actually a turn in Lampasas to stay on US 281. I have been this way many times, and cannot imagine why I missed or did not remember this. Looked at my map. Caught a farm road that looked like it was going in the right direction.

A couple miles down the road I came upon a Ford pickup with a flat. It was driven by a young woman, and she had her infant son with her. She had the truck jacked up and the spare out, but she could not get the lug nuts off the wheel. Seems to be my day for women in distress. I could tell the arrival of a 300-pound leather clad biker dude made her more than a little nervous. It happens. I introduced myself and offered her my phone. That made her more comfortable, even as she held up her own phone and said, "No service out here." Her name was Joyce.

The lugs were tight. Even by my standards. I had to put the truck back down so the wheel would not turn and I could apply a little "force of Danny". I bent the tire-iron getting the last one loose. That elicited wide-eyed, childlike admiration from Joyce. Apparently she likes watching guys bend tire-irons. Glad I could help.

Yep…It's all connected.

The farm road curved around a bit, then hit TX 29. I headed west on that to Llano. A 50-mile detour, but it was a great day for it. What's 50-miles give or take, when you are on a motorcycle?

Gassed up again in Llano. Caught TX 16 to Kerrville. Topped off "The Dragon" again in keeping with my general principle of having the machine always ready to leave if needed, and headed for the Kerrville-Schreiner State Park. Checked in, paid my fee, and went to find Wayne.

The park is a nice one, situated right beside the Guadalupe River, and just a couple miles out of Kerrville. In this gorgeous weather, with the impending weekend, it was inexplicably deserted. Wayne's big red Dodge was easy to spot in the otherwise empty park, even if his very nice dressed XS Standard had not been sitting there. I am afraid to ask how he managed to unload it out of his truck by himself...obviously he is capable. Wayne is a big guy too.

I set up camp, and cleaned some of the bigger bugs off "The Dragon", all the while shooting the breeze with Wayne.

We passed a pleasant afternoon, talking about bikes, trips, and other things. When nobody else showed by 7:00pm, we took off for town to find some dinner.

Wayne kind of randomly spotted/chose a Mexican food place, and we went inside. Turned out to be the site of the Friday dinner for the Valkyrie rider's group that was also in town, so we joined them (actually were kind-of herded into the room with them by the restaurant staff). I knew some, and we met others. I tipped the waitress pretty good, ostensibly because she was putting up with a bunch of biker types with good humor. Yeah, that was it, couldn't have had anything to do with her tight shirt and ample cleavage. The male brain, *sheesh!*

After dinner, we headed back to the campsite, to find that "Shack" had shown up. Shack had trucked his XS in from Nacogdoches and apparently arrived very shortly after we left for dinner. We helped him unload his very nice Special, and passed the evening in pleasant discussion around the campfire. We were expecting at least one more but he had not arrived. Phone service was sporadic at best in the area, so we were not sure what had happened. Of course we know from corresponding with him on the lists, that he can take care of himself, so we were not overly concerned.

Eventually we hit the hay, we were meeting any other XS'ives at a café on Main street for breakfast and to stage the day's ride early in the morning.

The night was cool and quiet, and my dreams were typical for when I am traveling on the Valkyrie. I am probably a psychiatrist's dream with my dreams! This one involved "The Dragon" in her dream form and me in mine. You will have to read *Hell and Gone*…all of it…if you would know what I am talking about.

I dreamed of dragons and unicorns, horrendous storms, pretty Texas women, and a whole world full of empty roads that always lead somewhere interesting, but never quite where I expect them too…

Saturday:

The morning dawned cool, crisp, and clear. A better day for riding has never existed. The three of us managed to get our act together and get to the café. There we met what was to be the rest of our group. Robert and Linda on their XS Standard, and Mike on his XS Special.

Two Specials, two Standards, and my Valkyrie. Looks like that debate will not be settled soon (of course Midnights Specials like "Well Oiled Machine" are just better!).

After a very good breakfast (eggs, pancakes, sausage, and hash browns for me) we prepared to ride. Amazingly enough, while we were gathered around the bikes, a very nice red and black XS Standard went cruising by. Alas, he did not see us. Perhaps we should have chased him down. Join the XS group or else! Well, maybe not.

We mounted up and headed for the hills. Ranch road 337 and 336 were the highlights of the trip. Up, down, and twisties. Scenery too! There are some big ranches out here—big money, old money, oil money, drug money, or maybe all of the above. Some certified nuts too, as one quite large ranch we saw was surrounded by a large white brick wall, which was topped on its entire length by broken bottles! Oh well, to each his own. Of course I was tempted to shoot the bottles off the top of the wall, but I suppose that would have attracted the wrong sort of attention. I'd have gotten off though, I mean, I am a Texan, what else are you supposed to do with a bottle sitting on a wall?

I rode sweep (the last rider's position) for the majority of the trip. There is something extremely satisfying watching all the bikes line up and sweep into the corners. Fortunately no wrenching or first aid talents were needed today. The bikes all preformed flawlessly, and the riders all had a good time.

We stopped for lunch at a very inexpensive and tasty hole-in-the-wall Mexican food place where we managed to totally bamboozle (technical term) the waiter. He was thoroughly confused from the word go. But they were nice enough folks and the food was quite good.

Shack is a character (of course all XS'ives are), and at one gas stop, he looked earnestly at Wayne and said "I am only getting about 47 miles to the gallon, something must be wrong!" That Shack…almost started a gas, oil, tire, and standard vs special argument right there at the gas pumps!

A stop or two for gas and drinks, and a full day of gorgeous riding, and back to Kerrville we went. Playing in those hills is a must-do. The last time I ran these hills was in the middle of the night, and not entirely voluntarily (see *SPI Bike Fest*). Daytime is so much better. I'll be back. Hopefully with a pack of XS'ives.

Back into Kerrville we went for a few pictures at the campsite. Then we regrouped for dinner, and cruised to a good steakhouse (not the one we were looking for, but a good choice nonetheless…holistic navigation again).

Good bikes, good food, good people. Makes for a good day, yes?

Back to the campsite the three of us went. Wayne was pulling out early in the morning, allegedly around 4:30am, and Shack figured he would too, so we loaded their bikes into their trucks so they would not have to do it in the wee hours. We then spent a couple hours shooting the breeze around the campfire.

The Park cop guy, with his cute flashing light adorned pickup was making a point of wandering around the park, and stopped to tell us that "quiet time" was from 10pm to 6am. We did have the radio on, very low, but were not really making any noise. Certainly not any noise that compares to driving a pickup all over the park. I think I startled my fellow campers with my urge to tell him, "Well, shut the hell up and get out of our campsite then."

I am a bit of an anarchist I suppose. *Sigh.*

The cool night air was perfect for sleeping.

So I did. My dreams this night are best left unrecorded. I am a passionate man, I'm pretty sure some of the things I dreamed are physically improbable—and possibly illegal—and my wife would blush.

Zonk.

Sunday:

I awoke at about 5:45am. Who needs alarm clocks while camping, when you are equipped with the boon of all tent campers...the 7-hour bladder.

Dressed and found to my surprise, Shack sitting in his truck. I gathered Wayne was down at the restroom facilities. I knocked on Shack's window, "What happened to 4:30am?"

He laughed, "Don't know."

I could have told them...there is really no such thing as 4:30am. Really. It is a myth that has only been sighted by a few unverifiable types. Its existence has never actually been proven.

I missed Wayne as I hiked down to the facilities, they were gone when I returned. I silently mouthed a heartfelt, "Godspeed." I like riding, I like people, and had met more people that I like, and the riding has been sheer joy. Wayne and Shack are good guys, Robert and Linda are very nice people, and Mike the Nasa Engineer has been charged with getting me a warp drive to install in "The Dragon". The world is good.

The fire was still smoldering, so I chucked the last log on it and brought it back to life. I sat in the cool predawn silence watching the crackling flames and contemplating. Other experiences, different trips, other times, other people, friends and lovers, present and those that have been lost, slowly come back to me. Life, death, joy, pain, all of it real, some of it very up close and personal. They are all there, and all can bear scrutiny on a morning like this one. All have left their mark, for good or ill, on my self and my soul. Some are deep and painful, others joyous, some simply fleeting contacts, but all very vivid, and continually shaping who and what I am, even when I am not sure myself what that is.

I end up staring intently into the flames, examining old pains, reconciling them with the joy and magic I know are prevalent in the world. Old scars, both real and mental are, one by one, dragged into the open and experienced yet again. People I know. People I have lost. People I have somehow affected. All are met, known, lost, or affected yet again. Slowly integrating, balancing, fusing my experiences, good and bad, with my self and my soul. Sitting there with tears unabashedly running down my face, yet tremendously, strangely elated.

I am who I am, I do what I do.

Yah. It's all connected. Slowly I smile.

The resounding, echoing, joyous, whooping, "YAHOOOOO!" I sent reverberating around the forest as I jumped up to break camp probably violated the "quiet time" but I grinned broadly when it was promptly answered from across the grounds by a female voice echoing the same sentiment. Apparently I am not the only one for urr…quiet reflection in the predawn light.

Mounted up and ready. The cool morning air was exhilarating, infusing my whole being with exhilaration and desire. A deep breath or two and I was ready.

I grinned, "The Dragon" roared, and we were gone.

The trip home:

I stopped for breakfast in Kerrville...I intended to go to the place we ate at yesterday, but it was closed Sundays. No problem. If you ever need breakfast in a small Texas town, and it is actually early, here is what you do. Drive up and down the main drags (and one street each side of the main drag) and look for all the pick-up trucks. Wherever they are, there is a good breakfast to be had.

Sure enough, pancakes, sausage, bacon, eggs, and iced tea. Waitress that calls everybody "hon". Six bucks including tip. Yum.

I headed out of Kerrville on TX 16, bound again for Llano, where I would make the cut back over to US 281.

I entered a really odd fog just north of Interstate-10 and stayed in it for miles. It was almost surreal, the sun was up and the fog was only at ground level. Visibility was only about ¼ of a mile, but within that circle it was sunny and the visibility was crisp.

This gave the very strong illusion that I was not moving at all, rather that I was stationary, and things were moving into and out of my sphere of being. I have ridden many thousands of miles, and this is the first time I have ridden in conditions quite like this. From my perspective, the world did not exist outside my sphere of influence, and all the things (like many, many deer) were simply created in front of me, moved silently behind me, and then were destroyed as they vanished.

Eventually a Harley rider was created in front of me, and as he slowly slid backwards toward me, he moved over to share his lane with me and waved me by. As I paralleled him for a moment I looked over at him, to find him looking at me. I am sure I was wearing the same ecstatic grin on my face that he had on his. A mutual thumbs up, and I pulled away in front. It was almost with regret that I let him vanish in the mists behind me.

Just short of Llano I topped a rise and the mists vanished. They did not fade away, lingering here and there, or simply become less solid until not noticed anymore, they vanished within the blink of an eye.

Quite startling really. I was suddenly back in the universe again. Not entirely sure if that is a good thing, but at least the deer were not "popping" into existence in front of me anymore.

This entire trip, I had seen very few cars, trucks, or bikes once I was away from the towns. I owned the road. One of the reasons I love touring. On one lonely stretch I overtook a white Chevy "whatever", one of those nondescript cars. As I passed the car I glanced over. A young lady was driving, and in the back seat was a youngling in a car seat. He was maybe 2 years old or so. He was flipping me off—as in, shooting me the bird. Waving at me with one finger for all he was worth.

My only thought, *Well…there's something you don't see everyday.*

As I pulled around, the mother glanced over at me, then into the back to see her son's greeting to the 300-pound motorcycle guy. She was obviously horrified, and nearly ran off the road. I chuckled to myself and drove on.

I stopped for gas, a coke, and a stretch at Hico. As is my habit, I fueled the big cruiser first, then pulled off the pumps into the shade in front of the store. I went in and got a diet coke, and as I was leaning against the bike sipping it, who should show up but the mother of the one-finger-salute kid. She had not seen me parked on the other side of another car, and walked around the car and right by me. She looked up and gasped, went completely white, and nearly passed out!

The kid's finger is on a aluminum splint, seems he got himself into a little trouble as young boys are wont to do…I reassured the nice lady that some motorcycle gang was not going to come rumble on her over this. Kids are universally cute at that age, and nobody with any intelligence is going to be riled over the actions of a two-year old. There is no animosity there. Heck, adults flipping me off don't even bother me.

People are funny.

Since I had fueled in Hico, I had no real physical need to stop in Glen Rose, as it is only about 30 miles up the road…except that I did need to stop, I wanted to check on Lisa. I pulled into the same station, being careful of the odd concrete edge this time, stuck my credit card into the pump (it was working this time) and put a bucks worth of gas, all she would hold, in the Valkyrie. I pulled off the pumps, and as I got off "The Dragon", Lisa burst out of the store carrying a Diet Coke, ran around several other customers, and gave me a flying bear-hug with all four limbs (she jumped and I caught) and a resounding kiss on the cheek. Good thing I am the big guy that I am, otherwise it would have been an enthusiastic tackle! Urr...good thing I have a strong heart too...that kind of thing will really get it going.

I grinned, "Hi Bob! You ok?"

"I knew you would be back this weekend! That's the only reason I am working...so much has happened! I am so excited! You were right! Oh thank you so much."

I extracted myself, "I take it that is a yes?"

With what seemed to be a bit of ceremony, she handed me the coke. "This is for you...Oh yes! Everything is great." She looked me in the eyes a moment. "I am going to be ok. Just like you said."

At that she flashed a smile at me, turned, and ran into the store. Somebody's worldview had shifted.

All she needed was somebody to care.

As I stood there sipping my coke, undoubtedly with a big grin on my face, the two Harley riders that had been fueling up walked by. One of them looked at me, glanced at my hard won coke and asked, "What do I have to do to get service like that?"

I am sorry. I could not resist. As I saluted him with the coke, kind of tipping it near my forehead, I said, "Just buy a Valkyrie."

He looked at the gleaming cruiser for a moment. Nodded, "Well, she is a nice bike."

I grinned, "The Dragon" roared, and we were gone.

Around 900 miles driven. Great roads discovered, new friends met, new experiences consumed. Riding, music, people. Man, road, machine, and soul all reaffirmed.

All-in-all, a pretty good weekend.

But…"The Dragon" is still calling.

Motorcycle Voyaging

Standing in the shade in front of the store, leaning on my massive F6 Valkyrie cruiser (nicknamed "The Dragon") and drinking a Coke, I was approached by a total stranger asking questions. This is a common occurrence and is one of the reasons I enjoy voyaging on the motorcycle.

"Where are you from?" asks the stranger.

I actually live in Garland, but most folks do not know where that is. Since it is a suburb of Dallas, usually I just say "Dallas", as people tend to recognize where that is without further information. With this person, I could tell any answer I could give was pretty much irrelevant. There was much more to the question than had been vocalized, and this person wanted to talk. I chose the long answer.

"I'm from Garland." I took another sip of my coke, awaiting the inevitable next question.

While somewhat hungrily eyeing the Valkyrie, the stranger let out a long sigh. Then, "Wow. I wish I had the balls to go cross country on a motorcycle."

I almost snorted the soda out my nose. Despite all my experience, people have an almost infinite capacity to surprise me, and today was demonstrating this yet again.

Shortly the speaker stopped looking at the Valkyrie and looked at me, suddenly realizing what had been said. I have never seen anyone blush so fully or so fast.

I was probably blushing too, as this speaker was a petite redheaded, green-eyed bombshell of a woman. She was about 4'6", and extremely well proportioned. She was wearing a low-cut tee shirt and tight blue jeans, and radiated her gender much like a space heater puts out heat. Anyone that is anywhere near her, has no choice but to notice her.

I am a lot of things. Sometimes I am not even sure what, but I have always been sure of one thing; I am unabashedly and un-apologetically male. I am not the slightest bit embarrassed about it so I will admit that the first thought that had popped into my head was that it would be a terrible shame if she ever managed to acquire the...ur...equipment...that she had so bluntly expressed a desire for. That conjures up visions even I do not want to see, so the next thing my male brain ordered up was a completely involuntary scan of the subject from top to bottom. Yep. Sexuality present and confirmed. Definitely a redheaded bombshell. *Yum.* I *do* love America.

I actually managed not to make any embarrassing comments and we began discussing long-distance riding. The conversation intrigued me, redheaded bombshell not withstanding, because I have heard other riders, men and women alike, express the same concern. We spent a few minutes discussing this, and I think she understood in the end.

Voyaging is not a matter of fear or bravery, balls, kahunas, guts, or any other equipment, gender-related or not. Six-foot, 300-pound, hairy-chested biker-looking dude, or four-foot six-inch redheaded, green-eyed bombshell, or anything in between, if the desire is there anyone can voyage. Voyaging is an attitude, plain and simple. Anybody can have it, anybody can do it.

I briefly reflect on the difference I find between those who go, and those who don't. It revolves around a couple similar, but markedly different definitions:

Voyage: A long journey to a foreign or distant place.

Voyaging: The events of a journey of exploration or discovery.

I am never on a *voyage*, whatever my destination. I am *voyaging*. I am not just trying to get somewhere. There are faster, cheaper, and more comfortable ways to do that. I am after the experience.

Voyaging has always been important to me. Transportation to a destination is not the purpose. There are faster and more comfortable ways to just get somewhere. I like seeing new things, meeting new people, and simply absorbing the experience of the ride. Distance riding can be at times uncomfortable. Rain, wind, dust, intense sun, heat, and cold, are all possibilities on a ride. The discomfort is usually temporary, and with the right attitude, will not even be remembered after it is gone.

I have long since ceased to worry about a mechanical breakdown. Should I breakdown, I will fix it, push it, junk it, or call for help. Or maybe even walk. Getting lost is not a worry. It is simply a new opportunity to see some new things, discover new roads, and meet some new people. I have also found that drivers are usually more aware away from the cities (there are exceptions, remain alert), and that I have much more fun if I stay off the super-slabs for the most part. Small towns are interesting places. Gas stations at towns that are outside easy commuting range of a big city are inevitably crossroads…for the routes people are traveling, as well as for events in their lives.

Riding sensitizes you to the machine you are astride, the road, and the sights and smells around you. I can smell the cars that have a smoker in them—cigarettes and other things too—even at 70 mph. I can smell perfume or cologne as the car containing the odorous individual drives by. Out in the country, I can smell a major city from 150 miles away. Due to the heightened sensitivity I am usually aware of any problems my machine has, long before they will affect me.

Riding organizes the mind and crystallizes the thinking. Self-reflection becomes important, and the time for that is needed, especially in today's world. Deep thoughts and revelations are easily possible, and if I am getting away from the cities, my entire perspective can change.

As I mounted the Dragon the redhead smiled at me once again. She seemed to understand herself, and maybe us males, just a little better. She may have gained a little confidence, and attitude too. As she climbed into the mini-van she was driving, she looked back at me sitting on my Valkyrie. She glanced at her van, then back at "The

Dragon" and said with smile and a gleam in her eye, "It really is all about what you have between your legs, isn't it?"

With that she was gone.

Sitting there, with the superb machine rumbling beneath me, I thought briefly of all the places "The Dragon" has carried me, and all the people that I have met while *voyaging*. I smiled and said to myself, "Yeah...Yeah I guess it is."

I grinned, "The Dragon" roared, and we were gone.

Today I Met a Man...

It only took a millisecond to register.

I hate to shop, but sometimes a man's just gotta. Stepping out of the store with my hard-won Christmas present for my wife a terrible scene lay before me.

My first and unbidden thought was, *Somebody's going to die!*

My second thought was, *Somebody's going to $#$#*%@ die!*

"The Dragon" was down you see. The big cruiser was laying on her right side, a bit of gasoline running across the asphalt. Standing over her in an incriminating manner was a teenage boy.

Let me start by stating that Valkyries do not just fall over. Period. She weighs 775 pounds dry, and she has a serious lean into the kickstand to prevent falling over even if both tires go flat. It would take serious winds to blow her over, and even with the stand up she will sit on her crash bars without falling unless she is pushed.

I am a Texan, and can be absolutely ruthless when needed, but I am slow to anger and must be seriously provoked to warrant a violent response.

I step out of the store and find a baggily clad teenager fooling with my fallen bike.

This was serious.

I was provoked.

I saw stars.

Somebody was fixing to die.

Still, I have been around enough to know that everything is not always what it seems to be in this world. Very little is black and white, or even gray, and while stereotypes and statistics can be highly accurate when applied to groups, they breakdown with spectacular rapidity when applied to individuals. I have also been judged incorrectly by people who do not know me or what I am about enough so that I am wary of jumping to conclusions. Benefit of the doubt and all that.

Good thing I do not shoot first and ask questions later.

I quickened my pace, headed toward the fallen bike and her unsavory teenage companion. For those that do not know me, I am 6 feet and 300-plus pounds. I am strong as an ox and supremely confident, and it usually shows in my walk and my manner. I can really move when needed. In this instance I was also dressed in my heavy leathers, the jacket alone weighing in at over 30 pounds. I am a BIG guy.

I have no idea what my expression was, but I am sure it was scary. I was pissed! My Dragon was fallen, my comrade was down!

About this time he looks up and sees me coming. Trust me, the better part of valor here would be to run and never look back.

His expressions went through an interesting range of emotions. Surprise, disbelief, panic, and outright terror rapidly crossed his face. His mouth dropped open and he actually blanched. I have never seen anyone go so white, so fast. His tongue and lips even went white!

I could see it in his eyes, he just knew I was going to pound him flat.

Then it happened. His arms tensed, his eyes rolled back—just a bit, he swayed, and his knees buckled—just a bit. He kept to his feet and recovered quickly, but not quite fast enough. A small wet stain soaked the crotch of his baggy blue jeans.

All this was observed in a matter of seconds. He recovered quickly. *But he did not run.*

I stopped an arm's length away. I could have reached out with one hand and throttled the boy. I knew it, and he knew it. He kind of squinted, looking a bit away, a hand half raised—the posture almost involuntarily taken a split second before a person gets clobbered by something. I would imagine that everyone that has ever been hit by a Mac truck looked like this a split second before impact. *And still he did not run.*

Clearly all was not what it seemed to be here.

"Explain yourself." It was all I trusted myself to say.

He knew he was going to die. His voice quavered, but he could look me in the eye.

His name was Shawn, and he and two friends were shopping. When they backed out of their space, they barely bumped the Valkyrie. Bad driving, and really annoying, but nothing sinister here. She went over and sat on her right crash bar.

Shawn (who was not driving) got out of the car and asked for help righting the bike. His friends laughed, and the driver backed up a little more, and over she went. Now we are into sinister. They then drove off, leaving Shawn to fend for himself.

Shawn tried to right the big cruiser but could not, so he waited for me.

He waited for me. He did not run.

Where I had seen just a boy when I came out of the store, I now realized that standing in front of me, quivering knees and all, was a man.

I turned the wheel to its stops and put my butt into it. Up came The Dragon. That is one heavy bike.

She had sat mostly on her soft saddlebag and the right crash bar, and the only damage I could find anywhere was the right rear blinker lens was cracked, and the front brake lever was bent. Not too bad.

I handed him my helmet. He was under eighteen after all. "Come on Shawn, let's go for a ride."

"Yes sir."

A quick trip to the gas station, and a stop at the Honda dealer later we were at Shawn's house. "That's them." Shawn said pointing to a white Honda Accord.

They had figured he would run, and were waiting for him at his house. Some friends.

I knocked on the door and things were sorted out in quick order. I can see where Shawn gets it from. His father is a man too.

He rapidly had the "friend's" parents over and we all had a little pow-wow. The driver was Terry, and his parents were furious with him. The end result was that I was given $50 cash for my expenditures ($47 or so) at the Honda shop, and then I was handed the keys to the Accord by Terry's father.

He said, and I quote, "The car is yours. Do whatever you want with it. Give me ten minutes and I'll have the title over here for you."

And then, "Do you want to swear out a charge?"

I looked at him a bit surprised, "What?"

Turns out Terry's dad is a cop. Oooooooooh, bad for Terry.

I looked him in the eye, "You'll take care of this?"

"Oh yes." There was no doubt at all in that tone.

I handed him the keys to his son's car.

"Okay then. Have a good one."

As for Shawn, well, I shook his hand.

He is, after-all…a man.

Conclusion

Roaring along at over 70 mph, "The Dragon" and I were well in tune with each other. The big Valkyrie cruiser had become an extension of my being. Over the last hundred miles bone, blood, muscle, and machine were somehow connected, together becoming much more than the sum of their parts. Together we flew almost sensuously through the evening light.

Other than the pleasure of the ride itself, this trip had been uneventful. That mattered little. I twisted the throttle and laughed as with a surge of power we shot up the long rise in front of us.

Cresting the hill, something caught my eye and I became suddenly alert.

Oh my...

My heart raced. Hitting both brakes and downshifting, I steered "The Dragon" off the shoulder, scattering gravel and dust as I went. I continued braking, pushing the superb machine right to the edge of her performance, and slid to a halt at the very peak of the hill. I had to take two long, deep breaths before I could totally absorb what I was seeing.

The vista spread before me was incredible—absolutely breathtaking. I was on the top of a ridge, with a broad valley spread out before me. Directly in front of me the sun was setting behind a huge thunderstorm, rendering it in dark, ominous purples and intense blood reds. There were at least a dozen rainbows within view. Lighting was striking with such frequency that it was almost constantly alight beneath the storm, and the rain and wind patterns could be clearly seen there. Tendrils of clouds writhed and twisted as they extended under the storm. Pre-tornadic and absolutely hypnotic.

Just over the crest of the hill, the road I was on forked. One side veered to the right and avoided the storm completely. A friendly ray of sunshine lit the way. By contrast, the other fork veered to the left and went directly into the heart of the storm. The landscape under the storm appeared to be only grays and blacks due to the stark and dramatic effect of the frequent lightning.

I frantically groped for the camera, afraid to take my eyes off the spectacle in fear of it vanishing. I snapped off several frames, while already knowing that the attempt to capture this was futile. I have taken many pictures on my rides, some of which are incredible, but all pale in comparison with the experience in person. As gorgeous as they can be, the pictures just do not quite grab the feeling or the *scale*. I do keep trying though.

Sitting there on the rumbling motorcycle, it forcefully struck me that the vista in front of me was very much like life. Clearly in front of me were choices and apparently obvious consequences. The motorcycle was part of it also. It represented free will. The freedom to take risks, the ability to choose, the avenue for experience, and the desire to dream. In front of me, two paths were presented, the easy way and the hard way, the light way and the dark way, the right way and the wrong way. My will, my choice, would carry me there. *But which was which?*

One way was an easy and short ride home, the other was directly into the jaws of the maelstrom in front of me, and then on into the unknown beyond it. To the right, a known road and an easy arrival at a destination. To the left, experience and a journey into the mysterious darkness and turbulence of the storm.

For me the choice was already made. I put the camera away and smartly zipped up my leather jacket. "Let's go girl." I said as I slapped "The Dragon" on the tank, and roared back onto the road. As I approached the fork and made my choice, I could feel "The Dragon" surge with raw power, adding her approval of my decision.

As we entered the storm and the rains and winds began to lash out at us, I smiled...a dangerous smile. The howling increased in intensity, and suddenly I realized I had added my own voice to that of the storm's. Life is amazing. Experience, both good and bad, is the purpose. The journey *is* the destination. Guts, faith, and soul cannot shield me from all the pain, but they *will* carry me through. I laughed and twisted the throttle once more.

I grinned, "The Dragon" roared, and we were gone.

Life is a road, the soul is a motorcycle.

About the Author

Daniel Meyer is a pilot, engineer, skier, and above all, an avid motorcyclist with a few hundred thousand miles under his belt. When asked to describe himself, his usual answer is, "I'm a six-foot, three-hundred pound, blue-eyed Texan; supremely confident and strong as an ox, though I usually don't smell like one."

0-595-26990-7

9 780595 269907